SPIRITUALITY
— *by the* —
NUMBERS

Also by Georg Feuerstein

Voices on the Threshold of Tomorrow
(edited with Trisha Lamb Feuerstein)

Holy Madness

Encyclopedic Dictionary of Yoga

The Yoga-Sutra of Patanjali

Introduction to the Bhagavad-Gita

Enlightened Sexuality

Sacred Sexuality

Forthcoming works

In Search of the Cradle of Civilization
(with Subhash Kak and David Frawley)

The Mystery of Light

SPIRITUALITY

— *by the* —

NUMBERS

Georg Feuerstein

A Jeremy P. Tarcher / Putnam Book
published by
G. P. Putnam's Sons
New York

A Jeremy P. Tarcher/Putnam Book
Published by G. P. Putnam's Sons
Publishers Since 1838
200 Madison Avenue
New York, NY 10016

Jeremy P. Tarcher, Inc.
5858 Wilshire Blvd., Suite 200
Los Angeles, CA 90036

Published simultaneously in Canada

Library of Congress Cataloging-in-Publication Data

Feuerstein, Georg.
      Spirituality by the numbers / by Georg Feuerstein.
          p.   cm.
      "A Jeremy P. Tarcher/Putnam Book."
      ISBN 0-87477-765-8 (alk. paper)
      1. Numbers, Cardinal—Religious aspects.   2. Spirituality—
Miscellanea.   3. Religions—Miscellanea.   I. Title.
BL65.N86F48   1994   93-47197 CIP
291.3'7—dc20

Design by Tanya Maiboroda

Printed in the United States of America
1   2   3   4   5   6   7   8   9   10

This book is printed on acid-free paper.

This book is warmly dedicated to
Lama Shakya Zangpo,
mentor and spiritual friend,
who is an old hand at cross-fertilizing
conceptual frameworks.

~ CONTENTS ~

~ PREFACE ~

Many, though by no means all, spiritual traditions have arranged their teaching concepts into meaningful *numeric* groups. Some of these groupings, such as the ten commandments of the Judeo-Christian tradition, the five pillars of Islam, and the eightfold path of Buddhism, are known to hundreds of millions of people. Other doctrinal sets have been the privileged knowledge of a few initiates—that is, until modern scholars rummaged around in their sacred literature, translated venerated esoteric texts, and made carefully guarded secrets readily available to the lay public.

True initiates seldom feel threatened by this exposure of their mysteries, for they know that the quintessence of their teachings remains hidden to all but those few who have ears to hear and eyes to see: those who are brave enough to embark upon spiritual life and discover its secrets and glories for themselves. But I believe it is useful to communicate what can be communicated, for one never knows which words will penetrate through to the heart and launch a person on a spiritual voyage or provide encouragement and support.

This book offers the discerning reader a colorful cross section through a range of spiritual paths, both of bygone ages and the present time. It illuminates how various cultures have conceptualized the sacred dimension and sought access to it.

This work is not about numerology or number symbolism, though some of the conceptual groupings treated are clearly charged with symbolic significance. I have indicated this but have not focused on it, because the objective of this book is to highlight the most important or fascinating doctrines and practices that have been grouped into numbered sets by various spiritual traditions.

When Jeremy Tarcher invited me to write this book, his suggestion was simply to include those matters that I considered relevant and enjoyable to write about or read. After a few detours, which proved useful learning experiences, this is essentially what I did. The present book, then, is not intended as an encyclopedic treatment of conceptual groupings within various spiritual traditions; for that I would have had to write several thousand pages. The material I have included is very selective and in many ways unashamedly idiosyncratic.

The book covers the best-known groupings, such as the two beasts of the Apocalypse, the Christian Trinity, the four cardinal directions in various traditions, the five elements in Chinese thought, the seven psychospiritual centers (*cakras*) in Tantrism, the ten commandments in the Judeo-Christian tradition, the twelve tribes of Israel, and so on.

It also includes many lesser-known groupings, such as the four steps to God in Sufism, the seven lights of the *Zohar*, the eight immortals of Taoism, and so on, as well as a few truly obscure groupings, such as the three old Gods of the Mayas, the Four Suns in the Native American tradition, and the five auspicious events in the life of an enlightened being in Jainism. This third category of entries seemed to me important to include for the insights that the selected items provide about vital aspects of spiritual life.

Together the groupings treated in this book offer a novel entrance into the essential core of the world's spiritual traditions. All this is placed in a larger context in the introduction. I believe that this book has achieved the original purpose set by my publisher: to inform and to capture the reader's imagination enough to want to probe further into the mysteries of the spirit.

I continue to be impressed by the tremendous ingenuity shown by my fellow humans in finding words for what is essentially (and often by their own admission) inexpressible, and for creating the gossamer frameworks that we call philosophies, metaphysical systems, or religious traditions. They are all attempts to make sense of human experience, both ordinary and extraordinary, and to give a deeper purpose to life.

The renderings from original scriptural sources are my own.

I hope that this book will stimulate and nourish the reader's own quest for meaning and purpose.

—*Georg Feuerstein*

~ ACKNOWLEDGMENTS ~

I would like to thank Jeremy Tarcher for the opportunity to roam freely in the world's gold mine of great and minor spiritual traditions and to find there the nuggets of wisdom contained on the following pages. His enthusiasm for the project and open-mindedness were manna from heaven for this writer's soul. Writing a book involves a kind of exodus, not unlike the Hebrews' migration from Egypt, which was the time when they were the happy recipients of divine nutrition. Each book calls for abandoning the relative security of the prison of familiar concepts and venturing forth into the wilderness of unexplored conceptual territory. The price of freedom is uncertainty—a negligible price to pay for so precious a gift. Besides, after every wandering, there is the reward of coming home enriched.

My thanks also go to my editor, Connie Zweig, for judiciously editing a text that turned out to be far more detailed than either of us had anticipated. I also would like to express my appreciation to Mel Ash and Roy M. Carlisle for suggesting a number of groupings, some of which I was able to include; and to Timothy Meyer for a superb copyediting of the manuscript.

~ INTRODUCTION ~

So teach us to number our days, that we may attain a
wise heart.

Psalm 90:12

If I could write the beauty of your eyes/And in fresh
numbers number all your graces.

Shakespeare, Sonnet 17

Better than a thousand useless words is one single
word that gives peace.

Dhammapada 8:1

FROM CHAOS TO COSMOS

When through the miracle of modern medicine sight is
restored to a person who has been blind from childhood,
something very curious but highly instructive happens.
When he or she first looks out onto the world, the visual
field contains no human faces, no trees, no houses, no
clouds—nothing at all. More precisely, it contains no
things. What the individual experiences instead is a "buzz-
ing confusion" of meaningless patches of colored light
and shade—a chaotic world.

Slowly patterns emerge that become recognizable
objects. But for a period of time these objects make no
sense, and the person must painstakingly learn to associate
them correctly with the information he or she receives

from the other senses. Thus the newly seeing individual gradually constructs the meaningful patterns that we call the universe.

The human mind's powerful pattern-making tendency has been studied by psychologists, who discovered that we tend to slightly modify the shapes we perceive to match the ideal forms that we entertain in our mind. We tend to ignore fuzziness and irregularity in favor of simplicity, regularity, and symmetry. We perceive in terms of *gestalten,* which is the German word for "forms." The same pattern-making habit is at work when on a sunny day we lie in the grass gazing up at the clouds and, in our imagination, detect all kinds of figures in them. Or when, as children, we saw monsters in the patterns of the wallpaper.

Human existence is inseparable from the search for, and maintenance of, meaningful patterns. As philosopher Michael Polanyi observed in his book *Meaning*: "Man lives in the meanings he is able to discern. He extends himself into that which he finds coherent and is at home there. These meanings can be of many kinds and sorts." We constantly make icons out of the reality we experience and, in turn, those icons fashion new icons out of reality.

Our icons do not necessarily match the icons carried around in the minds of our fellow humans. In fact, they are apt to be quite dissimilar in different cultures. As anthropologists have discovered, the human species sports a wide range of perceptual, affective, and cognitive styles. These styles are distillates of different ways of thinking and of *experiencing* reality.

The languages of the world faithfully reflect these often striking differences. They testify to the many ways in which we imaginatively carve up the universe we live in.

Sometimes, perhaps all too often, our constructions (interpretations) of reality are so divergent that communication between people collapses—not because vocabulary and grammar are different, but because the way in which reality is perceived and experienced is so irreconcilably distinct.

THE SPIRITUAL TRADITIONS AND
GLOBAL HUMANITY

Today, largely because of electronic communication and high-speed travel, the cultures of the world are in constant and intensive dialogue with one another. We are learning about each other's differences, rather than merely reacting to them with fear or incomprehension. Indeed, as the cultures of the world become more interdependent economically and politically, our survival as a species depends on our conscious effort to understand each other's interpretations of reality, or cosmologies.

Studying the world's spiritual traditions, both past and present, is an important aspect of this endeavor. Science- and technology-oriented materialistic ideologies are very recent and by no means flawless products of the pattern-making mind. They were preceded by thousands of years of visionary philosophy that interpreted the inchoate patchwork of light and shade in quite distinct ways.

Nor is this visionary approach—which we can call broadly spiritual—obsolete. On the contrary, materialistic interpretations of reality are limited to a comparatively small number of people, who look to the scientific priesthood for explanation and comfort. The overriding majority of the earth's population—even in the "materialistic West"—adheres to a more spiritual outlook on life. There is also no indication that future generations will be more "scientific" and less "religious" or "spiritual."

It is important to realize that both scientific and religious or spiritual world-views are *interpretations* of reality, not reality itself. Both are ways of finding or creating meaningful patterns that can guide us in the business of daily living.

Scientists and scientophils like to point to the success of science (through the medium of technology) as a sure indicator that the scientific world view is more correct than traditional religious cosmologies. After all, it was science that put human beings on the moon, discovered nuclear fission, and cured many previously incurable diseases. But it is also science, or its misguided use, that today threatens the survival of the human species and all life on this planet.

On the other side, of course, religious cosmologies have been the source of persecution, inquisitions, crusades, wars, and untold suffering. But they also have provided humanity with its noblest ideals and purposes. How much poorer we would be without Buddha, Mahavira, Krishna, Lao-tzu, Confucius, Moses, or Jesus of Nazareth? To this day, their teachings give meaning and spiritual sustenance to billions of people.

THE NUMBERS GAME

The spiritual traditions have much in common—conceptually and on the level of ritual and social practice—but they also differ from one another in often fundamental ways. Each tradition has its own reading of the human situation: the purpose of life, the path to be walked, and the goal to be attained. It is fascinating to see how the thinkers of these traditions—whether intellectuals or visionaries—have experienced and analyzed reality.

A recurrent motif in these spiritual cosmologies is the grouping of significant aspects of spirituality into numeric sets. Thus we have the Chinese metaphysical polarity of *yin-yang,* the three levels of afterlife in Christianity, the four goals of life in Hinduism, the ten biblical names of God, the twelve signs of the zodiac (which had more than mere astrological significance), the thirty-two secret paths of the Kabbalah, the sixty-four *yoginis* of Tantrism, the six hundred and thirteen commandments in Judaism, and so on.

Perhaps the teachers of the spiritual traditions have grouped basic notions into numeric sets because this assists the brain to remember teachings more readily. But it is impossible to say why the creative minds of a tradition create the numeric groupings they do, other than that, within their overall cosmology, these clusters tend to make sense. However, apparently some traditions favor enumeration more than others. This fondness for categorizing things and inventing numeric sets seems particularly present in the great spiritual traditions spawned in India: Hinduism, Buddhism, and Jainism. The first two are best known in the West, and consequently I have drawn from them more liberally than from Jainism or some of the other traditions.

I will discuss them shortly, but let's start with the more familiar terrain of Judaism and Christianity. The Jews have shown a fondness for number symbolism and numeric sets ever since the days of Moses. Thus, the first book of the Torah, Genesis, begins with the story of God's creation of the world in seven days. In the same book, God is depicted as instructing Noah to prepare for the Flood by building an ark and stocking it with all kinds of creatures "by sevens." In a later section, Genesis tells how Abraham offered seven ewe lambs to Abimelech when both entered a covenant, and how Egypt experienced seven years of plenty and seven years of famine.

The number seven occurs again and again in the Bible, as do the numbers four and three. Symbolically, four stands for the earth (the cardinal directions), while three represents heaven. Seven, which is the product of four and three, stands for completeness or wholeness.

The fourth book of the Old Testament is called Numbers, though its Hebrew title is *Bemidbar,* meaning "in the desert," which accurately describes the book's content. It relates the escape of the Hebrew tribes from Egypt and their years of wandering in the Sinai desert. The English name, which is derived from the Greek title *Arithmoi* (Latin *Numeri*), refers to the sections that give population figures for the various Jewish tribes.

The Jewish penchant for numeric sets and symbolic numbers reached its peak in the Kabbalah, the mystical tradition within Judaism. Among the most prominent sets are the ten *sefiroth* of the Kabbalistic tree, the thirty-two secret paths, and the seventy-two triplet letters forming a magically potent name of God (said to have been used by Moses to achieve the parting of the Red Sea when the Hebrew tribes fled from Egypt).

Each letter of the Hebrew alphabet has a numeric value as well. Thus the entire Torah (the first five books of the Old Testament) can be translated into the language of numbers. Some believe that the numbers reveal the hidden code of the Torah: God's message to the Jews. For instance, the letters in the Hebrew spelling of Yahweh (Jehovah) yield the number 26, whereas the symbolic number for

Adam is 605, for Eve 19, and so on. By means of this symbolic (numerological) method, which is known as *gematria,* Kabbalists look for meaningful correspondences between words that have the same numeric value in the hope of obtaining clues about the encoded message.

In Christianity, we find that the gospel writers hardly indulged in the number game, though they had a preference for the number seven and its multiples, mentioning the seven loaves that fed 4,000 people, the seventy-seven times a Christian should forgive another, the seven brothers who were married to the same woman, the seventy men who cast out devils in the name of Jesus. The preference for sets of seven was recognized in the twelfth century by John of Salisbury, who wrote a book entitled *De septem septenis* ("On the Seven Groups of Seven"), in which he explains the many heptads (groupings into seven) that fascinated the scholastic mind in medieval times.

Special mention must be made of the 153 fishes "in the unbroken net" mentioned at the end of St. John's gospel and the 5,000 people who had come to hear Jesus speak and were fed by him with only five loaves and two fish out of twelve baskets. As I will show, these two numbers conceal profound geometric symbolism, illustrating the close connection between spirituality and cosmography in ancient times.

Within Christianity the enumerating tendency found its most exaggerated expression in the Book of Revelation, or Apocalypse, ascribed to St. John. This work brims with number symbolism—most of it quite obscure—and has served as the basis for a flood of more or less speculative commentaries, both ancient and modern. Again the number seven features prominently in the list: the seven spirits before the throne of God, seven stars, seven golden candlesticks, seven lamps before the throne, the lamb with seven horns and seven eyes, seven seals, seven trumpets, and so on. Perhaps the most notorious of the symbolic numbers is 666, which stands for the Beast—often thought to refer to Nero, but also attributed to Stalin, Hitler, Mussolini, and other evildoers in history. The British occultist Aleister Crowley proudly claimed the title for himself.

The third great religion of the Middle East, Islam, also favors certain numbers and numeric sets, notably groups of five. Thus there are the five pillars of the Muslim faith, and the ritual prayer is performed five times a day. Traditional Islamic law recognizes five basic categories of action, namely obligatory, recommended, indifferent, disapproved, and prohibited. According to some Muslim schools of thought, there are five saints, which perhaps reflect the five members of Muhammad's household whose names are inscribed in amulets to this day. Finally, Muhammad is regarded as the fifth and final lawgiving prophet, preceded by Noah, Abraham, Moses, and Jesus.

The number seven likewise has special meaning for Muslims, notably Sufi mystics. To mention but a few examples, pious pilgrims must circumambulate the Kaaba in Mecca seven times and, as part of the pilgrimage, call out "God is great!" (*Allahu akbar*) seven times, and near Mina shower the Devil with three times seven stones. Furthermore, Muslim tradition speaks of seven cardinal sins and of seven inner aspects of the Koran.

The Sufis know of seven *lata'if,* which are energy centers in the body similar to the Hindu *cakras* upon which concentration is practiced. The mystical literature of Islam also mentions seven candles, seven spiritual robes, seven degrees of the spiritual hierarchy, seven primordial fountains, seven heavens, seven earths, seven spiritual leaders (*imams*), and so on.

When we turn to India, we find that Jainism—which is older than Buddhism—is especially fond of enumerations. This is strikingly evident in the *Tattvartha-Sutra* ("Aphorisms on the Categories of Existence"), which is a comprehensive manual of Jaina doctrines. This scripture was authored by Umasvati some 1,800 years ago, but its teachings are much older. Umasvati mentions group after conceptual group for easy memorization of the complex Jaina metaphysics and spiritual practice.

Thus he defines the two kinds of speech (thinking and verbalization); the three components of the path to liberation (right vision, right knowledge, and right conduct); the five kinds of knowledge (sense-based knowledge, scriptural knowledge, direct knowledge of matter, direct knowledge of other minds, omniscience); the six existential categories (soul, matter, virtue, vice, space, and time); the seven principles (soul, nonsoul, flow of karmic matter, bondage, stoppage of karma, shedding of karmic matter by the soul, and liberation); the nine principles (the preceding seven principles plus merit and sin), and many other sets, including the twelve forms of meditation, the fourteen levels of spiritual development, the sixteen actions leading to the formation of an enlightened being's body, the twenty-five kinds of activity, the 108 kinds of dependence on the soul (which are symbolized in the 108 beads of the Jaina rosary), and the 8.4 million types of embodied beings.

Buddhist authorities, too, favored numeric categorizations. The Buddha himself created the most important numeric groupings: the three types of suffering (suffering arising from pain, from change, and from inner causes); the four noble truths (existence as suffering, desire as the cause of all suffering, the elimination of suffering through the conquest of desire, and the eightfold path as the means to conquering desire); the five groups of grasping (body, sensation, perception, cognition, and consciousness); the six sense organs (the five senses and the mind); the noble eightfold path, and the twelve links of dependent origination.

Later teachers, in the Hinayana, Mahayana, and Vajrayana (Tantric) traditions, added many other sets. The Buddhist canon is arranged into three "baskets" (*pitaka*), or collections. One contains the disciplinary rules, another contains the Buddha's sermons, and the third collection is made up of various scholastic works. The Buddha's sermons are organized into five compilations that clearly show the Buddhists' flair for numeric assemblages, because the sermons are arranged according to their length (long, medium-long, and short sermons being gathered into separate compilations) and according to the number of treated topics. In the fifth compilation, the sermons are simply grouped according to topics.

For our purposes, the collection of scholastic texts—*abhidamma-pitaka*—is of special interest. It contains works that elaborate on the Buddha's teachings in great detail, making extensive use of numeric classification. Here we find, for instance, that the category of "body" (*rupa*)—one of the five groups of grasping—has twenty-eight subdivisions, whereas that of "consciousness" (*citta*) has fifty-two. Moreover, the Theravada (Hinayana) Buddhists distinguish a total of eighty-nine states in which consciousness can appear.

The *abhidamma* teachings were further systematized

by the philosopher Aniruddha in a famous Pali compendium, the *Abhidammattha-Sangaha,* written probably in the twelfth century A.D. This entire work revolves essentially around the numeric classification of Buddhist doctrines.

Like the Jainas and Buddhists, the ancient Hindus also displayed a considerable fondness for numeric groupings. In the *Rig-Veda* ("Knowledge of Praise"), the cultural fountainhead of Hinduism, which is now dated back to the third millennium B.C. and earlier, we find number riddles that contain cosmological and spiritual knowledge—riddles that could only be answered by initiates.

For example, Hymn I.164 mentions the horse with seven names (the sun), the seven sons (solar rays), the seven-wheeled chariot (the six double months and one intercalary month) pulled by seven horses (solar rays); the seven portions (the year, solstice, season, month, fortnight, day, and night); the wheel of twelve spokes (the year of twelve months); and the seven threads (forms of sacrifice by which the cosmic order is maintained). It also speaks of the one—the sun—who has three mothers (earth, sky, and heaven) and three fathers (three forms of God Agni) and of the seven half-embryos (meaning unclear) who apportion the seed of the universe.

Hymn X.90, which is a eulogy on the Cosmic Man (*purusha*), refers to the seven enclosures and the thrice seven pieces of firewood by which the Cosmic Man is "tied up" as a sacrificial offering. According to some authorities, the seven enclosures are the seven Vedic meters or the seven shallow trenches dug round the fireplace. The twenty-one pieces of firewood are probably the twelve months, the five seasons recognized in India, the three worlds, and the single sun.

There are other riddles to be found in the *Rig-Veda*

and in the somewhat younger *Atharva-Veda,* involving other numeric sets, too many to mention here. Some of these sets were the basis for the later metaphysical systems of Hinduism.

One principal school of Hindu philosophy—Samkhya—even bears the name "numbering" because its conceptual backbone is the enumeration of the principles of existence (*tattva*). In fact, the Sanskrit word *samkhya* was originally applied by various schools of thought to enumerated sets of metaphysical principles, and only subsequently came to be associated with a particular system.

One of the early (preclassical) works of Samkhya philosophy bears the name *Shashti-Tantra,* meaning "Book on the Sixty," which is a reference to the sixty main topics discussed by the thinkers of this school of thought. In its classical form, Samkhya admits twenty-four categories of existence (those that define insentient Nature, or *prakriti*), with the twenty-fifth category being the transcendental Spirit (purusha).

THE PATTERN OF TIME: CYCLES AND CALENDARS

There is another aspect to the numbers game: Since time immemorial, humanity has tried to make sense of change, of the flow of things, or what we call time. Thus in the Stone Age, apparently more thoughtful individuals kept track of the moon's journey across the sky. By the time the early neolithic cultures emerged in India, Anatolia (Turkey), Mesopotamia (Iraq), and Egypt, considerable astronomical knowledge had been accumulated.

The ancients, it seems, were obsessed with the regularities of the "heavenly" world. Looking up they saw what seemed to them perfection in Nature's arrangements of the planets ("travelers") and the two luminaries. Their concern with the stars was not scientific in the modern sense. Rather, they considered the great cosmic pattern as a model to be imitated on earth—a sentiment that is epitomized in the occult maxim "As above, so below."

To live a good life, one had to emulate the harmony above, to follow the example of the gods and goddesses who animated the sun, moon, planets, stars, and constellations. The twelvefold zodiac is the distilled wisdom of countless generations of stargazers who sought to discover the will of the higher beings. Only the virtuous person could hope to be favored by the heavenly powers and perhaps, at the end of life, be welcomed into heaven.

The spiritual path is typically characterized as an adventure of ascent from earth into heaven. Jacob's ladder and the seven-storied Babylonian temples (*ziggurats*) are both archetypal images for this age-old shamanistic motif.

We must appreciate the tremendous visionary abilities of our ancestors. They had none of the restraints on "weird" inner phenomena that apply in our postmodern civilization. They believed as much in carefully observing celestial events as in routinely watching their dreams. They slipped easily into trance states, and talked with the gods and goddesses, angels and demons, and a host of other beings for which the rational mind has no room. From our materialistic perspective we are inclined to dismiss all this as hallucination. But when Westerners take the step of apprenticing with a shaman or yogi, they quickly realize that Nature is full of invisible powers and entities—invisible at least to the rationally overdetermined eye, but visible to the eye of the initiate.

From a traditional viewpoint, the destiny not only of individuals but of humanity at large is governed by the powers above. The great celestial cycles are expressed in the world ages, which show humankind as traversing a downward spiral of progressive moral decline—from the Golden Age to the Dark Age of our time. The sages and thinkers of ancient India were particularly adept at calculating those eras. They envisioned an endless repetition of cycles, each lasting hundreds of thousands of years. They viewed time as a demon, and existence in time as a painful burden.

Other civilizations developed similar ideas. The Maya, for instance, were so preoccupied with temporal rhythms that they felt it necessary to employ five calendars, each calendar capturing a different aspect of the cosmic pattern, as played out in human history. Thus the ancients developed unique numbered sets—the *manvantaras, yugas, kalpas,* and other large cycles, as well as the annual calendars—seeking to capture the workings of the cosmic clock.

THE MODERN CHALLENGE

Unless we arrogantly assume that our own modern point of view is the only true one, the only correct reading of reality, we are naturally challenged by the conceptual tapestries created by other cultures and traditions. To the degree that we can overcome snobbery and xenophobia, we can learn greatly from the ways in which other cultures and traditions have patterned reality. Their meaningful sets, or conceptual groupings—whether of objects in space or cycles in time—can shed light on our own cosmology and show up possible blind spots in our approach to reality.

The modern world has been described as a world of disappearing boundaries. But this may not be quite correct. Perhaps our boundaries are simply becoming more permeable. There can be more and easier traffic between different constructions of reality, different worldviews and cultures.

As political scientist Walter Truett Anderson noted in his book *Reality Isn't What It Used to Be,* it is desirable that we recognize our social constructions of reality, but we do not necessarily have to discard them: "The Wizard of Oz, upon being exposed as human, may still be a very good man; and the belief, tradition, value, religion, norm, or Constitution that stands revealed as nothing more than a social construct may still be a very useful item."

Today we are challenged to inhabit the world responsibly but lightly, and to appreciate that there are as many perceptions and viewpoints as there are human beings. We all see the world through our own specific lens. This need not necessarily be a complete disadvantage. On the contrary, it can prove a powerful evolutionary stimulus, for in order to meet the global difficulties confronting us we may well need to call upon the combined knowledge of humanity's lenses, the wisdom of the various cultures and traditions.

If, as the prophets of our era are telling us, we must learn to think globally, we must first of all understand ourselves. And to understand ourselves we must understand our colorful species and its tremendous variety of solutions to the problem of human existence: the many minor and major traditions. When we succeed in peering beneath the surface of each tradition, past doctrinal accretions, we may discover our common human destiny.

THE VOID IN VARIOUS TRADITIONS

Why is there something—rather than nothing? What is existence? What is nonexistence? How are they related to one another? Such questions did not always form an integral part of humanity's philosophical repertoire. For untold millennia our ancestors lived without the slightest inkling that there could be a counterpoint to existence, or being. Then suddenly, when a sufficient level of intellectual sophistication was reached, some talented minds thought of a radically new idea: that in addition to being there was nonbeing, the absence of all forms.

As far as we can tell, this striking discovery was made some 5,000 years ago by philosophical-minded visionaries. This occurred at the dawn of the Indian civilization when the wisdom of the *Rig-Veda* was still being orally transmitted. In this ancient hymnody, which is the oldest literary document in any Indo-European or even in any language, we find the following speculative verses:

> Then existence (*sat*) was not, nor nonexistence (*asat*);
> space was not, or the heaven beyond.
> What encompassed, where, who nurtured it?

What ocean was there, profound and unfathomable?
Then death was not, or immortality.
The confine of night and day was not.
Undisturbed, self-moved, throbbed that One.
Beyond that, other than that, was nothing.

The thoughts expressed in the so-called Hymn of Creation, which opens with the above two verses, represent an astonishing advance in philosophical abstraction. It was destined to become a central concern of subsequent metaphysical speculation in India, leading to the grand conception of the Buddhist *shunya* or "Void."

We are told that in the beginning, before creation, there was neither existence nor nonexistence. It requires a considerable leap of intuition to appreciate what this means. To be sure, the ancient composer of those poetic lines was a visionary for whom that indescribable One was a living reality.

It is clear from his verses that he envisioned ultimate reality not merely as an absence but as a singular presence beyond all characteristics, or in which all possible characteristics coincide. It is the *potential* ground for all subsequent manifestations.

When the anonymous composer of the Hymn of Creation speaks of the imponderable reality as the One, he initiates a significant metaphysical trend that is characteristic of most Hindu schools of thought. Thus, many generations later, the anonymous author of the *Bhagavad-Gita* ("Lord's Song") has the incarnate God Krishna assure his royal disciple Arjuna of the following fact:

Nonexistence cannot come into being and existence cannot cease to be.

In subsequent centuries, Buddhist thinkers came up with their own ingenious way of talking about that which is really unutterable and indefinable. Refusing to refer to that intangible reality as "the One" (*eka*), they spoke of it as "the Void." Interestingly enough, however, the Sanskrit word *shunya* is derived from a root that can mean both "to be empty" and "to be swollen." Many archaic words have this built-in ambivalence. And this ambivalence can be detected even in the most radical schools of the Shunya-vada branch of Buddhism.

Gautama the Buddha preached that the goal of human life is to attain *nirvana*, the extinction of all ego-driven impulses. He also maintained that there is very little one can say about this extraordinary condition, other than that it is like waking from a long dream. Westerners have often misunderstood this spiritual ideal, confusing it with total annihilation.

Subsequent generations of Buddhist thinkers were less cautious in their statements than the founder of their spiritual tradition. Thus mainstream Mahayana Buddhism elevated the Buddha to the status of a deity and populated the heavens with numerous transcendental bodhisattvas. Nirvana was reinterpreted to mean merging with the Absolute—a notion similar to Vedanta but unthinkable in the context of early Buddhism.

About a hundred or two hundred years before the Christian era, some Buddhist teachers reacted against this trend. Picking up an earlier idea expressed in the Buddhist canon, they emphasized shunya, the voidness or emptiness of things. They went even so far as to dismiss then current notions of the Buddha—the path and nirvana—as being void or insubstantial. This radical position was systematized in the late second century A.D. by the philosopher and dialectician Nagarjuna, one of the finest minds of the ancient world.

Nagarjuna's intellectual labors notwithstanding, the idea of shunya was gradually reworked and equated, along idealistic lines, with the One Mind (*eka-citta*). Clearly, the whole notion of sheer nonbeing is difficult to sustain, no doubt because spiritual experience suggests something else.

In China, it was Lao-tzu who most memorably expressed the idea that the Ultimate, which he called the *tao* ("way"), was the unmanifest source of creation. In his *Tao Te Ching* (I.1–2), composed 2,600 years ago, he declared:

> The *tao* that can be expressed
>   is not the everlasting tao.
> The name that can be named
>   is not the everlasting name.
> Nonbeing (*wu*) is called the origin
>   of heaven and earth.
> Being (*yu*) is called the mother
>   of ten thousand things.

In verse IV.1, Lao-tzu speaks of the tao as "emptiness" (*ch'ung*). In Chapter 11, he offers the following similes: Without an axle-hole a wheel would not be a wheel, without a hollowed-out interior a vessel would not be a vessel, and without cut-out doors and windows a house would not be a house. Similarly, nonbeing is crucial to being.

Struggling to further explain the inexplicable, Lao-tzu remarked that, if pushed, he would describe this nameless something, which is "no-thing," simply as *ta,* meaning "great." But ta also means "passing on," and it means, paradoxically, "returning."

Turning to ancient Greece, we find the philosopher

Parmenides, similar to the God-man Krishna, rejecting the whole notion of nonbeing by postulating that reality exists and is singular. Democritus, who lived in the fourth century B.C., found the static philosophy of Parmenides unsatisfactory. Unwilling to deny the reality of the world of changeable forms, he postulated the existence of a void—empty space—which is filled by countless indivisible parts, or atoms. Ever since Einstein and quantum physics, we know that Democritus was wrong. There is no true vacuum, because space is filled with radiant energy.

For the same reason, the Christian doctrine of creation out of nothing (*ex nihilo*) is unconvincing to modern science. Yet the biblical account of creation is, strictly speaking, not arguing in favor of nonbeing. After all, creation presupposes the existence of the creator. It was through Yahweh's fiat that the cosmos sprang into being. He existed before all else.

However, the Buddhist notion of shunya has its parallel even within Christian monotheism. In the thirteenth century, the German theologian and mystic Meister Eckhart spoke of the Godhead as a pure nothing. He held that the divine essence transcended the trinity of Father, Son, and Holy Spirit. But he also taught that the Divine is pure "isness" (*istigkeit*) and that, by comparison, all manifest things were sheer nothing. Not surprisingly, Eckhart got in trouble with the Pope. But for the same reason that brought him close to excommunication, Eckhart appealed to the leading Zen master and scholar D. T. Suzuki who found many Zen-like elements in Eckhart's sermons.

In most other traditions, the problem of creation has been tackled in a different way. Thus, many mythologies conceive of creation as an act of self-sacrifice on the part of the original being, the primordial Person—the One.

THE ONE IN VARIOUS TRADITIONS

Our senses present to us a world of infinite variety, and we experience the universe as a composite of countless discrete objects. By habit we think of ourselves as separate individuals confronting this highly differentiated cosmos, as if each person were a unitary self. At times of personal crisis, when we inspect ourselves more closely, we find that we ourselves are actually a collage of subpersonalities. It is our memory that provides us with a sense of inner continuity.

In contrast to this common experience of multiplicity, the spiritual traditions of the world affirm that there is a state of being that is truly unitary, cohesive, unfragmented, whole. It is frequently referred to as the One or the Singularity. This idea is beautifully captured in the following line from the ancient *Rig-Veda*:

The bards have many names for the One.

The One is considered to be the atemporal and aspatial origin of all manifestation. It is equated with the

Divine, the Godhead, the Absolute prior to all differentiated forms.

Metaphysicians and sages of all cultures and eras have puzzled over the relationship between the One and the Many, the world of plurality. They arrived at many diverse and sometimes even contradictory answers.

Some think that only the One exists and that the Many is simply an illusion. This point of view is commonly called "monism" (from the Greek *monos,* meaning "singular").

Others, like the Neoplatonists, maintain that both the One and the Many are real, but that the Many emanated out of the One and continues to subsist in the One.

A third group speaks of the world having been created by the One but not containing the One in essence. To this camp of interpretation belong the great monotheistic traditions of Judaism, Christianity, and Islam. They postulate a big chasm between the Creator and his creatures.

A fourth group entertains the view that the Many is as real as the One, but there is no connection between them. This dualist metaphysics is characteristic, for instance, of the Samkhya system and the school of classical Yoga, according to which there are two eternal transcendental categories—the conscious Self (*purusha*) and insentient Nature (*prakriti*). The manifold universe is thought to flow out of the latter principle, whereas the Self remains forever on its own and only deems itself implicated in Nature until the moment of enlightenment. Moreover, there are many such Self-monads. A similar view is put forward in Jainism.

It is the transcendental Singularity, exceeding the senses and the mind, which the *philosophia perennis* deems the most worthy target of human attention and intention.

It is the *summum bonum,* the ultimate good, the "highest" reality. The spiritual traditions imply that the One, though lying beyond the ken of the intellect and the senses, can in fact be *realized.* In the Christian tradition this realization is referred to as *unio mystica,* or mystical union, yielding the unitive consciousness in which everything is experienced as the One.

In the Kabbalah, the mystical branch of Judaism, the One is known as the *ain sof,* meaning "that which is without end." This hidden reality is infinite because it is pure, singular Being. This notion of the Divine as an apersonal reality contrasts with the orthodox Hebrew view of Yahweh as the Creator God who is forever beyond his creatures.

When Muslims pray to Allah they pray to a God who, in the words of the prophet Muhammad, is "the One, Allah the eternally Besought of all," who "begetteth not nor was begotten" (*Koran,* sura 112). Every day, pious Muslims repeat the ritual formula: "There is no deity except Allah." The name "Allah" is commonly derived from *al* ("the") and *i'lah* ("God"). Thus, Allah is *the* God, *the* One.

The idea that the ultimate reality is singular is fundamental to all monotheistic faiths; hence the designation "monotheism," which is derived from the Greek words *monos* ("singular") and *theos* ("God"). It is often contrasted with polytheism, which is the belief in the existence of many Gods. On closer inspection, however, many so-called polytheistic traditions are found to believe in an ultimate Singular Being after all, which presides over the lesser deities.

For instance, the Australian Aborigines, whose religion has often been branded as primitive animism, believe in an All-Father prior to manifestation. Whereas creation results from the activity of the Rainbow Serpent, the All-Father—variously called Ungud, Mangela, Pundjel, and Baiame—is pure Presence impossible to describe.

Similarly, the Native Americans, whose belief system is sometimes described as "mere" tribal shamanism, believe in a supreme Being—the Great Spirit, or Creator. Thus, the Lakota know the Great Spirit, who is far superior to all other spirits, as Wakan Tanka ("Holy Great") and the Wind River Shoshoni as Tam Apo ("Our Father"). Ed McGaa (Eagle Man), an Oglala Sioux, writes in his book *Mother Earth Spirituality:* "The Indians knew the meaning of humility when they stood beneath the Great Spirit in ceremony and prayed. 'Oh, *Wakan Tanka* [Great Spirit, Great Mystery] make me worthy.'" And Petalesharo, a Pawnee Indian, summed up well the deep relationship of his people with the Divine when he said: "We love the Great Spirit."

~2~

THE TWO PRIMORDIAL POWERS
IN ZOROASTRIANISM

Zoroastrianism, the religion of ancient Persia, was founded by Zoroaster (Zarathustra), who is thought to have lived in the sixth century B.C. or earlier. He renounced the world at an early age and began to teach in his thirtieth year, living to the ripe age of seventy-seven. Zoroaster taught that opposing the "radiant, glorious, greatest, most beautiful, most perfect, and most bounteous spirit" of Ahura Mazda ("Wise Lord") was Angra Mainyu ("Angry Spirit"), the embodiment of evil. In the Parsi religion, which evolved out of Zoroastrianism, Angra Mainyu is known as Ahriman. Zoroaster preached:

> When these two spirits came together in the beginning, they established life and death. (*Yashna* XXX.3)

Even though existence is portrayed as a continuous battle between the two hostile forces of good and evil, Zoroaster made it clear that the good ultimately wins. The all-wise Ahura Mazda is the source of light, maintainer of the universe, and final arbiter of all destinies. So long as the universe exists, Ahura Mazda's power is limited by the presence of Angra Mainyu (Ahriman). However, at the end of time, when the cosmos dissolves again, the influence of evil is conquered and everlasting beatitude ensues.

The Zoroastrian idea of the co-existence of good and evil in the world greatly influenced the Gnostic schools of thought. We can also see its influence in Judaism (after the Babylonian exile), Christianity, and Islam in the notion of Satan, the eternal enemy of God.

The human being can freely choose between the power of Ahura Mazda and that of Angra Mainyu. The final consequence of one's choice is experienced upon death, when the soul crosses the "Bridge of the Separator." It widens for those who have chosen good, guaranteeing them safe conduct to the abode of immortality, but becomes narrow like a razor's edge for those who have foolishly opted for evil, hurling them into the abyss of eternal damnation.

THE COSMIC TWINS IN THE
NATIVE AMERICAN TRADITION

The ultimate Reality, whether conceived as Void or as One, is too ineffable for the human mind, which is designed for dealing with the world of multiple objects. However, many traditions envision an in-between state of polarity that is intended to explain the transition from the ultimate Singularity or Void to the countless things and beings of the manifest universe.

The mythologies of many American Indian tribes include a story cycle about the original Twins who claim more attention than the remote figures of First Man and First Woman.

Among the Keres of the Southwest, for instance, the original twins are two sisters—Uretsete and Naotsete. They are the first-born of creation and were sung into life by Ts'its'tsi'nako (Thought Woman), who is better known as Spider Woman. Before all creation, she chanted over the medicine bundles that contained the spiritual potentials of the Twins, thus breathing life into them. Uretsete later assumed male form—the kind of sex change not unheard of in mythology. Uretsete gave birth to twin brothers, one of whom subsequently married Naotsete.

The Navajo, the largest Indian tribe in the United States, also knows of Twins, whom they invoke in most of their ceremonies. The exploits of Monster Slayer and Child of the Water, which served the Navajo as models of conduct in war, are a constant reminder that manifest existence is a matter of creative conflict, or struggle.

THE TWO FORMS OF THE ABSOLUTE IN HINDUISM

Vedanta metaphysics, which lies at the core of many spiritual paths within Hinduism, is characterized by its nondualist orientation: There is only the One, which is known as *brahman*. However, the Vedanta philosophers and sages early on realized that the language of nondualism cannot account for the fact that the unillumined mind experiences a multiplicity of forms, which undergo change in the course of time. Hence they sometimes spoke of two types of brahman: the lower (*apara*) and the higher (*para*).

The Sanskrit word *brahman* stems from the verbal root *brih,* meaning "to grow" and also "to swell." Thus the term conveys the sense of infinite expansion, though it is always understood that the brahman ultimately transcends space just as it transcends time. The word is frequently rendered as "Absolute."

According to the early Vedanta thinkers, the world evolves out of the transcendental Singularity, and is in essence not different from it. This emanationism is the original form of Vedanta metaphysics. Later, sophisticated thinkers like Shankara sought to formulate a more self-consistent system. Wanting to safeguard the nondualist foundations of Vedanta, they explained all multiplicity as being the product of illusion (*maya*). Only the One is real, whereas the universe as we experience it is a phantom conjured up by our spiritual nescience. When we truly see what is "in front" of us, when we are enlightened, all multiplicity vanishes and only the transcendental Singularity remains. This metaphysical position is often referred to as illusionism.

However, Shankara insisted that the world exists so long as we are unenlightened. Upon enlightenment, it simply reveals itself in its true nature, which is brahman. Hence he had no difficulty retaining the earlier distinction between a higher and a lower brahman, and even to speak of a Creator. But he always made it clear that dualist talk is based on ordinary knowledge, which is inferior to spiritual gnosis.

Because there is only the one unsurpassable reality, we must necessarily be also identical with it. Hence the famous maxims: *aham brahma asmi* ("I am the Absolute") and *tat tvam asi* ("That art thou"). This equation of the Self (*atman*) with brahman is the basis for the spiritual path associated with Vedanta metaphysics. If our true nature is none other than brahman, then true knowledge consists in the peeling away of all false presumptions about oneself and the world. The Vedantic path is epitomized in the dictum *neti, neti,* "not this, not this." At the core of practical Vedanta is the consistent differentation between the ultimately real and the apparently real. This is known as the path of gnosis, or *jnana-yoga.*

THE TWO POLES OF THE ABSOLUTE IN SHAIVISM

The Middle Eastern religious traditions of Judaism, Christianity, and Islam speak of the Divine in masculine terms. In recent years, this theological habit has come under scrutiny as a result of the gender awareness created by the feminist movement. To conceive of the Divine as a male God has been shown to derive directly from the patriarchal social matrix of those religious traditions. As a growing number of historians are arguing, prior to the rise of patriarchal religions, the cultures of the Stone Age and early Neolithic revolved around the worship of the Mother Goddess.

In the spiritual tradition of Indian Shaivism, the gender issue has been resolved by regarding the Divine as the play of the bipolar forces of God and Goddess, Shiva and Shakti. Thus according to the philosophical Shaivism of Kashmir, the ultimate Reality comprises two aspects: pure Awareness (*cit*), in which there is neither subject nor object, and universal Energy. The former aspect is Shiva, the latter Shakti. The two are also respectively referred to as the transcendental and the immanent or creative aspect.

Shiva and Shakti are inseparable. Shiva without Shakti is said to be a corpse, and Shakti without Shiva is said to be devoid of light and delight, incapable of creation. In iconography, they are depicted as a male and female in intimate embrace. In Tibetan Buddhism (Vajrayana), such iconographic images are called *yab-yum*, meaning "Mother/Father."

This phraseology reminds one of the far older distinction, made by the Australian Aborigines, between All-Father and All-Mother (symbolized in the Rainbow Serpent). The creative tension between them can be said to be the trigger for the emergence of the manifest world.

Shiva and Shakti, like the All-Father and All-Mother of the Aborigines, are both precosmic (transcendental) and cosmic (immanent). They exist as one on the absolute level beyond space and time, and together they weave the space-time continuum with its infinite forms. But the cosmos is not merely created out of Shiva-Shakti, but contains within it that very Reality. The transcendental Shiva-Shakti is enfolded in the material universe.

This ultimate polarization of Reality is reflected also in the human body-mind. The Shiva pole is found at the crown of the head, and the Shakti pole is situated at the base of the spine. The basal pole is the seat of the *kundalini-shakti,* the "serpent power." According to esoteric anatomy, the *kundalini* ("coiled one") is the Shakti principle in the context of the microcosm, or the human body.

The purpose of *kundalini-yoga* is to awaken the dormant power of the feminine principle at the base of the spine, and to conduct it along the central axis to the crown of the head. There the dynamic kundalini energy merges with the masculine principle of Shiva, yielding a state of unsurpassable ecstasy. That blissful condition, in turn, transforms the human body, revealing it to be none other than the ultimate Reality of Shiva-Shakti.

THE TWO POLARITIES IN CHINESE METAPHYSICS

The human mind employs the principle of polarization to grasp the complex realities of existence. In fact, the brain has been compared to a binary computer operating on the basis of Yes/No, On/Off instructions. Thus we think in terms of such dualities or polarities as light and dark, good and evil, heaven and earth, birth and death. The Shiva-Shakti doctrine of some schools of Hinduism applies the same fundamental idea to metaphysics.

Frequently this polarization has been expressed in gender terms, as male or female. One of the most striking articulations of this is found in the archaic Chinese notion of *yin* and *yang,* captured in the *t'ai chi* symbol. This symbol is composed of two lobes forming a perfect circle. The upper lobe is black with a small white circle, the lower is white with a small black circle. This well-known symbol, suggesting a continuum, clearly shows the interdependence of both types of polarized energy.

These two poles are understood as the feminine and masculine principles that conjointly are responsible for the variety of forms in the universe. They are the engine behind all change. According to the *Li Chi* (Book of Rites) of Confucianism, yin and yang are the products of heaven and earth. As is clear from Lao-tzu's *Tao Te Ching,* however, heaven and earth spring from the nameless, everlasting tao.

The terms *yin* and *yang* originally applied only to "dark" and "light" respectively, but subsequently came to be used in reference to all forms of polarity or duality. Yin came to stand for softness, passivity, and contraction, and yang for hardness, activity, and expansion. Together they are considered the co-creative forces that shape the world (macrocosm) and human nature (microcosm). From their intermingling arise the five elements of material existence, which, in turn, are the source of the "ten thousand things."

The sixty-four hexagrams of the *I Ching,* an ancient divinatory book, are based on the two principles of yin and yang. Only two of the hexagrams are pure yin and pure yang, namely *k'un* and *ch'ien*; all others represent a combination of the two, representing the totality of manifest forms.

SEE ALSO The Eight Trigrams of the *I Ching*

THE TWO TYPES OF BUDDHIST NIRVANA

The Sanskrit term *nirvana* means literally "extinction," and it refers to the removal of all egoic desires in the condition of enlightenment, which is compared to the extinguishing of a flame. This state of "annihilation" is the avowed spiritual goal of all schools of Buddhism. The concept often has been misconstrued by Westerners to mean total extinction, which would give Buddhism a nihilistic outlook that it does not possess.

In the early Buddhist scriptures, nirvana is understood as a condition entirely apart from the human personality and the finite universe. In a well-known passage in one of the Pali sermons, for instance, Gautama the Buddha is quoted as saying that nirvana "is where there is neither earth nor water nor fire nor air . . . neither this world nor the other world nor sun and moon." In other words, nirvana exists, though it cannot be adequately described or grasped by the human mind.

No doubt in order to avoid misleading his listeners,

the Buddha preferred to speak of nirvana in negative terms. Thus he described it as "unconditioned" and "transmundane," and as being marked by the absence of all change. In his words, it neither arises nor ceases. It also is devoid of karma and rebirth, and contains no desire, delusion, or hatred. The Buddhist scholar Edward Conze was right when he observed that all conceptions about nirvana are misconceptions.

With the rise of Mahayana Buddhism, which emphasizes the unity of all things, the concept of nirvana underwent a reinterpretation. It became equated with *samsara,* the conditional world. According to the idealistic metaphysics of the Mahayana schools, transcendence and immanence are one and the same. Therefore, nirvana is not "somewhere else" and must not be aspired to outside oneself. It is innate in every being.

However nirvana is explained, its practical consequences are identical, for it spells the termination of all suffering (*duhkha*). From the viewpoint of Hinayana Buddhism, nirvana appears twofold. The nirvana attained during one's lifetime is known as "extinction with a remnant of conditionality" (*sopadhi-shesha-nirvana*). That which is attained after death is called "extinction without a remnant of conditionality" (*nirupadhi-shesha-nirvana*). The latter is also referred to as "complete extinction" or *parinirvana.*

In Mahayana Buddhism, this distinction assumed special significance, because the *bodhisattva* (enlightenment being") vows to postpone final extinction until all beings are liberated. This has often been interpreted to mean that the bodhisattva favors social action over enlightenment, but this would make little sense. The bodhisattva exerts himself to attain enlightenment precisely in order to be better able to help others. But his path is marked by compassionate action. Also out of compassion, the bodhisattva resolves not to abandon the world of form after he has attained enlightenment, but retains some kind of body (whether physical or energetic), so that he can continue to assist his fellow beings on the spiritual path.

The distinction between the two kinds of nirvana is similar to the distinction in Hinduism between "living liberation" (*jivan-mukti*) and "disembodied liberation" (*videha-mukti*). The nature of the realization is the same, whether or not the enlightened being has a body.

THE TWO ORIGINAL HUMANS IN THE JUDEO–CHRISTIAN TRADITION

According to the Judeo-Christian tradition, on the sixth day of creation, God fashioned a human male and a human female, together with all (other) animals. He called them Adam and Eve. From the union of this original couple our entire species, with its five billion individuals, is said to have derived.

According to the opening narrative of the Old Testament (Genesis 1:1–31), Yahweh created both male and female, fashioning them in his own image. A second creation narrative (Genesis 2:4–24), which probably belongs to the tenth century B.C., has Yahweh fashion first Adam's body out of a lump of earth. In fact, the Hebrew name *adam* means "earthling." Then he animated this body of clay by breathing the breath of life into its nostrils. He appointed Adam as his gardener in the special garden he had created east of Eden, the heavenly paradise.

Feeling that it is not good for a man to be alone, Yahweh made him a partner. He caused Adam to fall into a deep sleep, took one of Adam's ribs, closed the wound again, and then out of the removed bone fashioned the first female human, Eve.

The Hebrew name, from which "Eve" is derived, is *Hawwah,* which has been taken to mean "Mother of all living." But there is a more profound association in this name. The related Aramaic word *hiwya* means "serpent." This makes sense when we remember that it was Eve who listened to the serpent in paradise, consumed the forbidden fruit, got Adam to do the same, and thereby provoked God's anger. Throughout Christian history, Eve always has been portrayed as the original sinner. According to Muslim tradition, she was created out of the feet of the serpent.

When we look at these facts historically rather than theologically, we find that Eve reflects a wisdom tradition that preceded the patriarchal religion of the Hebrews and that involved magical ophidian (snake) rituals. This becomes still more obvious when we take into account the figure of Lilith in medieval Hebrew literature. Lilith ("Night Demon"), who is thought to have been created before Eve and who was responsible for Eve's seduction, is commonly portrayed as part snake. Some historians see in her a continuation of the neolithic Snake Goddess, which was the focus of fertility and sexual rites.

THE TWO ROADS IN THE
NATIVE AMERICAN TRADITION

According to Sioux tradition, the Great Spirit gifted the "two-leggeds" with all kinds of blessings to be able to honor life on earth. In particular, he taught that there are two roads—one red, the other black. Red is the color of the earth itself and, as Lame Deer observed, the blood and skin of his people. It also is the color of the peace pipe, a key implement in the ritual life of the Sioux. The red stone from which the peace pipe is carved is quarried at a sacred spot in Minnesota, the heartland of the former Sioux territory.

The red road is said to run from North to South. In Sioux cosmology, the North is connected with the color red, whereas the West is associated with black, since this is the place where the sun sets, giving rise to the blackness and mystery of night. The North is associated with clarity and purity, whereas the South is related to the source of life. The red road is thus the road of life, the "straight and narrow path" of the virtuous, those who know and re-spect the inner meaning of the peace pipe and the other sacred objects and rituals of the Sioux.

The black road, however, is the path of error and of moral and spiritual decline. The nineteenth-century Oglala medicine man Black Elk explained that this is the path of "one who is distracted, who is ruled by his senses, and who lives for himself rather than for his people."

A similar motif is found in the *Manual of Disciplines,* one of the Dead Sea (Qumram) scrolls thought to belong to the Essenes. It speaks of the way that leads toward God and the way that leads to damnation. One passage, trans-lated by Theodore H. Gaster, reads:

> Men have walked both in wisdom and in folly. If a man casts his portion with truth, he does right-eously and hates perversity; if he casts it with per-versity, he does wickedly and abominates truth. For God has apportioned them in equal measure until the final age . . . He will determine the fate of every

living being in accordance with which of the [two paths has been chosen].

The Essene idea of a dual way is echoed in the gospels of Matthew (7:13ff.) and Luke (13:23ff.). The former apostle reports Jesus as having spoken of the strait gate and narrow way leading to life and the wide gate and broad way leading to destruction.

The idea of the twofold moral option in life is also present in the *Yoga-Bhashya,* the oldest available Sanskrit commentary on Patanjali's aphorisms of Yoga, which was written in the fifth century A.D. Here it is stated that the "river" of consciousness flows toward the good and the bad. The good stream starts with proper discernment (*viveka*) and terminates in spiritual liberation; the bad stream begins with confused understanding and ends in bondage and sorrow. The bad stream is checked by means of the practice of dispassion (*vairagya*). The good stream is opened up by the practice of higher understanding arrived at through meditation.

THE TWO BEASTS OF THE APOCALYPSE IN CHRISTIANITY

The Apocalypse, or Revelation, of St. John the Divine belongs to the most obscure and fascinating portions of the New Testament. St. John was on the Mediterranean island of Patmos when he heard a loud voice behind him. It ordered him to write everything he would hear and see next. When he turned round, he saw the shining figure of the Christ, followed by a long and incredibly complex vision.

At one point, St. John saw a beast (Greek: *therion*)

coming out of the ocean. It had seven heads with ten crowned horns, and on each head a blasphemous name was written. It resembled a leopard, with feet like those of a bear, and a lion's mouth. The beast was empowered by a dragon standing on the shore. One of the heads, he noted, appeared to have had a fatal wound that had been healed.

St. John further saw how the people worshipped both the dragon and the beast, and the beast reigned supreme for forty-two months. It constantly blasphemed against God, and was even allowed to wage war against and conquer the saints.

Then he saw a second beast emerge from the earth. It had two horns like a lamb but spoke like a dragon. It exercised the authority of the first beast in its stead, and even worked all kinds of miracles. It deceived the people of the earth and tricked them into worshipping an image of the first beast. Those who refused to do so were killed when the second beast breathed life into that image, which then caused death and destruction.

Moreover, the second beast had the survivors branded with the symbolic number of the beast. Henceforth everyone bore the numeral 666 on the right hand and forehead.

Next, St. John saw "the Lamb," Jesus Christ, stand on Mount Zion with 144,000 saved souls, who had his name and "the Father's" name written on their foreheads. Then an angel declared the fate of those who had worshipped the beast: They would be annihilated with fire and sulfur.

St. John returns to the theme of the beast in a later passage where he describes how he was transported in his vision into a great wilderness. There he saw a scarlet beast with seven heads and ten horns. Riding on the beast was a harlot, dressed in purple and scarlet and adorned with gold, jewels, and pearls. The woman was drunk with the blood of the saints. She held a golden cup filled with the "abominations and the impurities of her fornication." On her forehead was written the name "Babylon the great, mother of whores and of the earth's abominations."

The angel who had transported St. John into that wilderness explained to him that he was seeing neither the past nor the present but the future, and that both woman and beast would meet with destruction. The woman, the angel explained further, is none other than the city of Babylon, described as "the great city that rules over the kings of the earth."

Since the historical city of Babylon had long fallen when St. John had his vision, and the vision itself was supposedly a glimpse of the future, we must look for a symbolic interpretation. Thus we may understand the two beasts as representing that side of human nature which has not yet been conquered by the spirit. The elements from which they arise, namely water and earth, are associated (according to Hindu esotericism) with the two lowest psychophysical centers of the human body, those regulating the eliminatory and sexual functions.

The dragon is the cosmic force of evil itself, or Satan. The beasts are depicted as being in the service of that principle. Babylon stands for fallen humanity, the man and woman who give no thought to God but spend their days and nights in the pursuit of egocentric goals. When Babylon has fallen, the holy city of Jerusalem, descending from heaven, will be established. Here Jerusalem symbolizes the spiritually regenerated human individual, and the purified human species as a whole.

For Christians, the coming of the Christ, which precipitates the fall of Babylon and the establishment of the new Jerusalem, has always been a concrete historical event in the future. However, we may understand this teaching in more universal terms, in which case it has relevance beyond the confines of the Christian tradition.

~ 3 ~

THE CHRISTIAN TRINITY

Christianity, together with Judaism and Islam, is one of the great monotheistic religions of the world. All branches of the rambling tree of Christianity subscribe to the fundamental belief that God is one. Thus, the Nicene Creed, which is an integral part of the modern eucharistic liturgy, affirms the existence of "One God the Father almighty, maker of Heaven and Earth, of all things visible and invisible."

To the puzzlement of many Christians and non-Christians, official Church doctrine goes beyond the simple affirmation of a singular Divinity. Rather, it recognizes a Holy Trinity composed of God the Father, the Son, and the Holy Spirit. How can the one God be three persons? Ever since early Christendom, theologians have demonstrated considerable ingenuity in trying to answer this question, employing logic, common sense, and at times hair-splitting to make their points.

The doctrine of the Holy Trinity was formulated to account for the historical fact of the Christ's incarnation, death, resurrection, and ascension, as well as the descent of

41

the Holy Spirit at Pentecost—all fundamental Christian beliefs. It was an effort to reconcile the paradox that the Christ, the "Son of God," was of divine origin yet embodied as a human being.

Originally, Christians had no collective name for the three forms of God. In the second century A.D., Tertullian invented the term "trinity." Eager to emphasize the unity of the Divine, the early Church Fathers regarded the three persons of God as merely temporary modes of a singular divine principle. Subsequent theologians found this solution unsatisfactory and engaged in rather sophisticated debates.

One of the great early Christian thinkers, Origen, who flirted with Platonism, proposed that the Spirit was subordinate to the Son and that the Son was subordinate to the Father. He looked upon the three as individuals, or what he called *hypostases*. Arius, on the other hand, believed that the Christ was indeed "begotten," as the Bible says, that is, the first creation of God. He, more than any other Christian theologian, came closest to saying that there is not one God but three divine persons. His ideas (sometimes referred to as "tritheism") were roundly condemned at the Council of Nicaea, which tried to secure the creed that the Christ was "begotten" but eternal and hence fully divine.

Centuries of debate and changing opinions followed, with theologians being reprimanded, chastised, and even anathematized for their views by Mother Church. The speculations of St. Augustine proved especially influential, though even he did not utter the last word in the matter, for the debate continues to this day. The most extreme position is represented by the Unitarians, who flatly reject the doctrine of the Trinity and revere Jesus as an inspired human individual.

The concept of the paternal Christian God has its roots in the figure of the Hebrew Yahweh, the heavenly Father. While Yahweh was conceived as an utterly transcendental being, he nonetheless was believed to have intervened in Israel's history. Through Abraham, Moses, and the other prophets, he made his will known to humankind. The Bible is deemed the Word of God.

It was God's "breath," the *ruah elohim,* that inspired and empowered the prophets in their role as religious and cultural leaders. This ancient notion is the starting-point for the later concept of the personalized Holy Spirit.

The second person of the Trinity is the Logos who was incarnated as Jesus of Nazareth. He addressed Yahweh as "Father" (*abba*) and also spoke of himself as the "Son of God." He was considered more than a man of God. He was in intimate filial relationship to the Divine or, as St. John put it, "in the bosom of the Father." In some passages of the New Testament Jesus the Christ is even considered "equal with God," "one with God," and "in the form of God." This is where Christians and Jews parted company.

THE THREE DIVINE FORMS IN HINDUISM

When we think of Hinduism, we think either of a pantheon of countless, many-armed deities or the singular Absolute of mystics, the *brahman.* However, Hinduism also has a quasi-trinity, which is indicated by the Sanskrit word *trimurti.* This term is composed of *tri,* meaning "three," and *murti,* meaning "form."

The trimurti is a metaphysical notion embodied in an iconographic image that merges the three great deities of popular Hinduism, namely Brahma (the Creator), Vishnu (the Preserver), and Shiva (the Destroyer). Artists have depicted this trimorphic Divine as a single body with three heads. Brahma is in the center, Vishnu on the left, and Shiva on the right.

The notion of a trimorphic Divine made its first appearance in the *Mahabharata,* one of India's two national epics. It played a prominent role in some of the *Puranas,* popular encyclopedia-type compilations. The trimurti appears to be an attempt to bring together the three major religious "denominations" within Hinduism: Vaishnavism (centering on the worship of Vishnu), Shaivism (revolving around the worship of Shiva), and nonsectarian Brahmanism. Brahma, who was the most abstract of the three deities, won few worshippers. Similarly, the Hindu triad—a product of theological speculation—never became a popular object of worship, though it is a pervasive symbol of Hinduism.

Sometimes the appellation "trimurti" is applied to three-headed depictions of Shiva, such as the famous stone sculpture of Shiva Maheshvara in a cave on the island of Elephanta in the vicinity of Bombay.

Beyond the three deities, the Hindu metaphysicians conceived of a formless reality, which they called brahman. This brahman (a neuter word in Sanskrit) is to be distinguished from the Creator-God Brahma (a masculine word). The brahman is the absolute Reality comprising all manifestation as well as all unmanifest and invisible levels of cosmic existence, including the various realms inhabited by the deities of popular Hinduism. The highest moral or spiritual goal of the Hindus is mystical union with the brahman, rather than Brahma, the Creator God.

Interestingly, the boundless and formless brahman itself is frequently said to have three aspects: being (*sat*), consciousness (*cit*), and bliss (*ananda*). Yet, these are not parts of a composite being, since the brahman is by definition "whole" (*purna*) and impartite.

THE THREE OLD GODS OF THE MAYA

The Maya of Mesoamerica created a truly astounding civilization whose roots date back to the second millennium B.C. Their religious beliefs and practices are still only poorly understood. It seems that they believed in a single ultimate principle, but also recognized a pantheon of many deities, though three gods appear to have held special significance for them.

At Palenque, a favorite tourist attraction in the Mexican state of Chiapas, archaeologists discovered a triad of old gods who were celebrated by the ancient Maya as the ruler's divine ancestors. The gods, whose exact names are not known, have conveniently been labelled GI ("G one"), GII ("G two"), and GIII ("G three").

The three gods were born eighteen days apart to divine parents whose birth occurred in the previous world cycle. GI, the first born, bears his father's name, though neither name has been deciphered yet. Apparently he is associated with the Hunapuh mentioned in the *Popol Vuh,* one of the few surviving manuscripts of the Maya. The glyph standing for GI consists of a highly stylized head of a man with a shaved pate, a Roman nose, prominent front teeth (often replaced by a shark's tooth), fish fins on the cheeks, shell earflares, and a curious headdress relating to the water-lily monster. Archaeologists think that god GI has strong associations with the Sun and Venus, whose courses in the firmament were closely followed and calculated with astonishing accuracy by the Mayan priests and timekeepers.

God GII is also known as God K, the Flare God, and the Manikin Scepter. He is depicted in a zoomorphic fashion, and his distinguishing marks are the mirror on his forehead and the axe puncturing the mirror, as well as the one foot that is transformed into a serpent. He was the third born of this strange triad. This god is especially associated with Mayan rulers and their ceremony of self-inflicted bloodletting.

God GIII, the second born, has been identified as the Sun God Ahau-Kin ("Lord Sun"). He is depicted as a human figure or a human head, with the numeral four (the sign for *kin*) being prominently displayed. Another distinguishing mark is his pair of squinting eyes. He appears to be associated with, or in some way identical to, the Jaguar God, a solar deity representing the sun in the netherworld of Mayan cosmology.

Another triad of deities is known to have presided over Xibalba, the nether region. They are depicted as toothless and wrinkled old men. Archaeologists have given them the names God L, God N (or Pauahtun), and God D (Itzamna).

In classical times, the Mayan kings would regularly undergo a bloodletting ritual, which was thought to sustain the gods. Thus the kings were caretakers of the deities, and the royal ritual undoubtedly also led to actual visions of the deities.

THE THREE BODIES OF THE BUDDHA

According to Mahayana Buddhism, Gautama the Buddha is not merely the historical individual who over 2,500 years ago renounced his royal heritage to assume the life of an ascetic, attained enlightenment after much inner struggle, and then taught others the noble eightfold path of the Buddha. Above all, the Buddha is the ultimate Reality, whether it be called "Thusness" (*tathata*) or "Emptiness" (*shunyata*).

As the ultimate Being, the Buddha is also referred to as the *dharma-kaya* or "dharma body." The Sanskrit term *dharma* has many nuances of meaning, which are not easily captured in a single English word. It is derived from the verbal root *dhri,* meaning "to bear" or "to support." It stands for the Buddha's liberating teaching, which supports the spiritual impulse in beings; it denotes the great order of the cosmos, which supports all of Nature's laws and regularities; and it signifies the ultimate essences or factors of existence, which support all composite things.

Thus the *dharma-kaya* is, first, the ultimate Reality itself, which is the support (dharma) of all manifest forms. Secondly, it is the Buddha's liberating teaching, which is the means by which others may similarly realize the ultimate Reality. Thirdly, it is the support of all dharmas or ultimate factors of conditioned existence.

Since the *dharma-kaya* is formless, it cannot be perceived by the senses or grasped by the mind. As the *Uttara-Tantra,* a third–century Buddhist scripture, declares:

> The ultimate Truth of the Buddhas
> can be realized only by faith.

Indeed, the sightless person cannot see
the radiant solar orb.

Faith is not the same as mere belief, but a deep inner
certainty based on direct intuition, which is the only portal
to the nondual formless Reality. Enlightenment, or liberation, is simply the realization that there is only the immutable *dharma-kaya* and that all phenomena are illusory. The
Buddha's earthly body—the *nirmana-kaya* or "transformation body"—belongs to the phenomenal level of existence
and hence is illusory as well. In truth, the Buddha was
never born and he never died, and his apparent attainment
of enlightenment was simply a "skillful device" (*upaya-
kaushalya*) to disrupt the spiritual ignorance of those who
deem themselves other than the one Reality.

Placed between the immutable *dharma-kaya* and the
Buddha's illusory physical body is the supramundane
sambhoga-kaya or "enjoyment body." This is understood to
be the conglomerate of all the transcendental bodhisattvas
in their "Buddha Lands," or pure realms of being. These
transcendental domains can be perceived only by those
who have reached the last of the ten stages in the life of a
bodhisattva. The human Buddha, who is remembered and
venerated as the founder of Buddhism, is in truth a conjuring trick created by the *sambhoga-kaya* out of immense
compassion for all self-deluded beings. But, like the
earthly body, the glorious *sambhoga-kaya* is also impermanent. Only the *dharma-kaya* is eternal.

THE THREE FUNDAMENTAL BELIEFS OF ISLAM

Islam recognizes three basic religious creeds, known as
usul al-din: The first creed is the belief that Allah, or God, is

one. This acknowledgment is known as *tawhid* in Arabic, which is derived from the verb *wahhada,* meaning "to make one" or "declare unity." God's absolute unity is affirmed in the declaration "There is no god except Allah." Sufis, representing the esoteric aspect of Islam, seek to realize that transcendental unity through mystical experience.

The second creed is the belief in the revelatory power of prophecy (*nubuwwah*), which ended with Muhammad, since the Koran is understood as the final message of God to humanity. Muhammad is considered a "prophet" (*nabi*), an "envoy" (*rasul*) of God, a "warner" (*nadhir*), and a "bringer of glad tidings" (*bashir*).

The third creed concerns the resurrection (*ba'th*) of the dead on Judgment Day when they will be either received into heaven or hurled into hell.

This triad of beliefs is common to all branches of Islam. However, the Shi'ah Muslims add two further creeds—the perfect justice (*'adl*) of God and the authority of the *imams.*

SEE ALSO The Twelve Imams of Islam

THE THREE TYPES OF HUMAN BEING
IN CHRISTIAN GNOSTICISM

One of the texts found near the town of Nag Hammadi in Upper Egypt in 1945 has been dubbed by scholars "The Tripartite Tractate." It deals at length with the Holy Trinity but shows a penchant for other tripartite conceptual groups.

Most fascinating is the division of humankind into three essential types, which are respectively referred to as the spiritual, the psychic, and the material. These types, which were brought forth by the Logos (the original Word), are said to have been unknown prior to the coming of the Christ.

The spiritual type is "like light from light and like spirit from spirit." When it emerged out of the Logos, it opened itself immediately to the "Savior," the Divine, in complete faith and thus received all revealed knowledge. Hence the spiritual type is destined to attained complete salvation.

The psychic type is "like light from a fire." When it emerged from the Logos, it moved toward the Divine hesitatingly and did not open itself fully to the revealed knowledge. It had to be instructed indirectly by a voice. Its destiny depends on the decision of the individual, who can choose good or evil.

The material type is "alien in every way." It shuns the light of the Divine, and therefore its destiny is complete destruction.

THE THREE TEMPTATIONS OF JESUS THE CHRIST

After Jesus was baptized by John the Baptist in the river Jordan, he went out into the wilderness, guided by the Holy Spirit. There he fasted for forty days. The story is told in the Gospels of Matthew (4:1–11) and Luke (4:1–13), with a brief mention in the Gospel of Mark (1:12–13).

During Jesus' forty days in the desert, the Devil appeared, asking him to demonstrate that he was indeed the Son of God. He wanted Jesus to turn stones into loaves of bread. Jesus responded with the famous words, echoing Deuteronomy 8:3:

50

. . . One does not live by bread alone, but by every
word that issues from the mouth of the Lord.

In the second temptation, the Devil led Jesus to the
rooftop of the temple in Jerusalem, inviting him to jump
off to demonstrate that his fall would be cushioned by
God himself.

In the third temptation, the Devil took Jesus to the
peak of a tall mountain, showing him all the kingdoms of
the world that could be his if only he were to bow down to
him, the Devil.

We can understand these temptations as having been
of a visionary nature in which Jesus confronted the darker
side of his own unconscious. The Buddha and Zoroaster
underwent similar testing. We know that all three found-
ers of religions resisted the Devil (the ego), affirming their
surrender to the spiritual principle.

After these trials, Jesus was ready for his great ministry that was to change the world. His forty days in the
wilderness remind one of the forty years that the Israelites
wandered in the wilderness after their exodus from Egypt
under Moses. Both periods were times of testing and trial.
The Israelites subsequently were led to the promised land,
and Jesus was allowed to commence his teaching.

THE THREE PRIMARY QUALITIES OF NATURE
ACCORDING TO SAMKHYA METAPHYSICS

In the early days of nuclear physics, physicists thought that
the fabric of the universe was composed of three types of
fundamental particles: protons, neutrons, and electrons.
Since then a whole "particle zoo" has been discovered (or

invented), consisting of a seemingly infinite number of hadrons. Feeling a need for simplicity, nuclear physicists pursued their experiments and came up with quarks as the ultimate building blocks of the cosmos. Thus today five distinct levels of (invisible) existence are recognized: molecules, atoms, nuclei, hadrons, and quarks. Many scientists suspect that their journey of discovery is not over yet.

But, for now, three kinds of quarks are inferred from experiments. These are picturesquely labelled "up" (or "chocolate"), "down" (or "vanilla"), and "strange" (or "strawberry"). There are also said to be three antiquarks, called "charm," "bottom," and "top" (which remains to be experimentally verified).

At any rate, we appear to be back to a tripartite model of the physical cosmos. This is quite intriguing, for already 4,000 years ago, India's thinkers and visionaries identified three fundamental forces of Nature. They called them *gunas,* meaning "qualities" or "virtues." The three types are *sattva, rajas,* and *tamas,* which stand for the principles of lucidity, dynamism, and inertia respectively. Sattva is that quality which underlies all those physical or mental things and functions in the universe that are illuminating, uplifting, or delightful. Rajas is responsible for whatever is dynamic, expansive, or simply agitated. Tamas is that essential quality which confines, delimits, or weighs down.

According to the philosophers of the Samkhya school of thought, a prominent school of classical Hinduism, the universe in all its dimensions is produced by the interaction of the three gunas. The gunas exist in varying mixtures, and are in constant oscillation and thus responsible for all the change we witness within and around us. Higher realms have a predominance of the quality of lucidity, lower realms are increasingly governed by the principles of dynamism and inertia. In our material realm, which the Samkhya philosophers consider to be a rather low manifestation, the principle of lucidity is only present to a weak degree.

It is the purpose of Samkhya—and also of the related tradition of Yoga—to cultivate the principle of lucidity within oneself through self-understanding and meditation. Through intensive spiritual work the mind can be progressively purified, until its sattva aspect is so predominant that the transcendental Self (*purusha*), or Spirit, is reflected in it without distortion. Then we come to know our true identity, which is the supraconscious Self.

The Self is *nirguna,* that is, it transcends the three qualities of the universe. It is always in a perfect state of balance. For the person who has realized the Self, the world "stands still," though for everyone else it continues to revolve unceasingly, causing anguish and predictable loss.

THE THREE WORLDS ACCORDING TO VARIOUS TRADITIONS

The idea that the universe is stratified belongs to the most ancient intellectual heritage. The Hindus, for instance, speak of the three *lokas:* the earth realm, the mid-region (or atmosphere), and the heavenly realm. The Sanskrit word *loka* stems from the verbal root *loc,* meaning "to be bright" or "to shine." This hints at the universal function of light, which is fundamental not only to perception but to objective existence itself.

Frequently the three worlds (known collectively as *tri-lokas*) are thought to comprise hell, earth, and heaven in ascending order. This notion is found in Hindu and Jaina scriptures, and we are also familiar with it from Hebrew, Christian, and Muslim cosmology.

In Buddhism, the phrase "triple world" (*trai-lokya*) refers to three levels of existence that can roughly be equated with heaven, as experienceable in deep meditation. The three realms are respectively called *kama-loka* ("realm of desire"), *rupa-loka* ("realm of forms"), and *arupa-loka* ("formless realm"). The Tibetans greatly elaborated on this, creating a complex edifice, with the thirty-three deities of the *Vedas* accommodated at the bottom of the heavenly realms and the primordial Buddha at the apex.

This kind of hierarchic arrangement is typical of most archaic cosmologies, which portray existence as a multi-layered structure that is topped by the heavenly domain. Each level, or dimension, has its own distinct population. The significant fact about the worldly realms—from hell to heaven—is that they are the playground, or battle ground, of the human psyche, affording it innumerable learning experiences. The implicit challenge is to recognize that there are higher realms to which one can ascend, if only in consciousness.

According to the mystical tradition, the task of the human psyche is ultimately to transcend all its world games and realize its essential unity with the Divine. The Divine (be it called "God" or "Self"), of course, is beyond all lokas. It is truly utopian or "placeless."

THE THREE CHARACTERISTICS OF
CONDITIONED EXISTENCE IN BUDDHISM

One of the important contributions of existentialist philosophy is the reformulation in modern terms of the ancient insight that we are beings who are always in passage. We are innately restless, constantly recreating ourselves by giving ourselves new goals. As Jean-Paul Sartre observed, we must constantly choose who we want to be, and this freedom of choice maintains us in a permanent state of anxiety.

Anyone who cares to analyze life deeply enough will come to the stark realization that we are indeed immersed in a rather strange or, as Sartre put it, an "unreasonable" situation. That situation had been spelled out with shocking succinctness 2,500 years before the renowned French philosopher. In his very first sermon delivered on the night of the full moon in July 528 B.C. after his spiritual awakening, Gautama the Buddha said:

> This, o monks, is the noble truth of suffering: Birth is suffering; old age is suffering; illness is suffering; death is suffering; grief, lamentation, pain, affliction, and despair are suffering; union with something that is not loved is suffering; separation from what is loved is suffering; failure to obtain one's desires is suffering.

In short, all of life is suffering for the Buddhist. This is the first of the three characteristics of conditioned existence. The second characteristic is that everything is tainted by the stigma of death and hence cannot afford us a haven of safety. The third characteristic is that all things lack a lasting essence, or self (*atman*). Thus, in summary, the three characteristics are suffering (*duhkha*), impermanence (*anitya*), and inessentiality (*anatman*).

In view of this teaching, Buddhism frequently has been viewed as vastly pessimistic. However, the Buddha did not stop there. In contrast to much existentialist philosophy, he also showed a practical way out of this dilemma, leading to nirvana.

SEE ALSO The Noble Eightfold Path of the Buddha; The Four Noble Truths of Buddhism

THE THREE LEVELS OF AFTERLIFE IN THE JUDEO–CHRISTIAN TRADITION

All religious traditions have provided their own distinct answer or answers to the question "What happens after death?" The question has lost none of its appeal, as is evident from the numerous books on the subject. Today thanatologists (death scientists) are trying to lift the curtain upon a mystery that previously was the prerogative of shamans and priests, visionaries and mystics.

According to Catholicism, there are three levels of afterlife existence. Those who obeyed God's will in life can expect to go straight to *heaven.* Sinners who have repented end up in *purgatory,* whereas the unregenerate sinners plunge headlong into *hell.*

The etymology of the word "heaven" is unclear. It may originally have meant something like "canopy," referring to the celestial vault. In religious terms, heaven is widely understood as the place "up above," that is occupied by the divine being or beings. The early Hebrews do not seem to have had a clearly articulated teaching about heaven, though this could merely be a sign of our ignorance of their beliefs.

The imagery of heaven was developed during the period of time between the conclusion of the Old Testament and the creation of the New Testament. Three, seven, or sometimes even ten levels of heaven, or paradise, were distinguished. God was believed to live in the highest heaven, but not be contained by it.

In the rich imagery of the New Testament, heaven becomes a place of bliss in which God's steadfast worshippers are eternally rewarded for their faith. Now heaven is also specifically associated with the Christ, who is said to have come from heaven and to have ascended to heaven after the resurrection.

Hell, the opposite pole to heaven, traditionally has been located below, under ground. The ancient Hebrews knew an underworld (*sheol*), where *all* departed spirits lived a shadowy existence, without either punishment or joy. Later they added the belief in a subterranean place of punishment for the wicked, called *gehenna,* which is also referred to in the Gospels. Those who enter hell are destined to remain there forever. Origen, an early Church Father, taught that the wicked and demons would ultimately be reintegrated and restored to God's favor, but the Council of Constantinople in 553 A.D. explicitly rejected this liberal view.

Little wonder that the threat of hell, the "place of tears and gnashing teeth" (Matthew), has instilled horror in the hearts of millions of Christians. Both priestly and popular imagination has run wild in picturing that abysmal place and the torments awaiting the wicked. One of the most imaginative portrayals can be found in Dante's *Divine Comedy,* where he distinguishes nine circles or levels of hell. Another equally picturesque account of hellish existence is given in Emanuel Swedenborg's *Heaven and Hell.* Swedenborg, who was considered one of the great mystical giants by Emerson, claimed to have had numerous visions of hell and heaven.

By most accounts, Christians can expect to do time

in purgatory rather than suffer eternal damnation in hell. The belief in purgatory does not seem to be spelled out in the New Testament, though from the beginning Christians have prayed for their dead. This custom makes sense only if it is assumed that prayers can make a difference to the departed. While those who have entered heaven are scarcely in need of assistance, all those souls who are in purgatory may be thought of as potential beneficiaries of the prayers and good thoughts of the living.

The Western Church tends to conceive of purgatory as a place of punishment and purgation, whereas the more contemplative Eastern Church sees in it rather a place of maturation and preparation for entry into heaven. In the sixteenth century, Luther—followed by Calvin and the Anabaptists—rejected the whole idea of purgatory and also of saying prayers for the dead. For Protestants, the afterlife is thus a black-and-white affair. One either goes to heaven or to hell.

Sophisticated interpretations of eschatology ("science of last things") understand heaven and hell as states of consciousness rather than locations. Heaven is the experience of the presence of the Divine, whereas hell is the self-chosen state in which one suffers separation from the Divine.

THE THREE PHASES OF AFTERLIFE
ACCORDING TO THE TIBETANS

The *Bardo Thödol* ("Liberation through Hearing in the In-between State"), better known as the *Tibetan Book of the Dead,* is based on teachings going back to Padmasambhava ("Lotus-born"), who in the eighth century A.D. established Tibetan Buddhism and founded the Nyingma sect.

The *Bardo Thödol* in its present form is a product of the fourteenth century. Originally serving as a manual for meditation, it came to be used for death rituals. It is recited for the deceased to give him or her the opportunity to go through the death process with full awareness and find a suitable place of rebirth.

According to this sacred work, the process of death and rebirth has three distinct phases. These are known as "transitional states," or *bardos,* which are understood to be states of consciousness.

In the first state, at the moment of death, the dying person comes face to face with the Clear Light. This supernal white light is a sign of the presence of the *dharmakaya,* the absolute "body" of the Buddha. The dying person is reminded to continue his or her meditation practice and merge with the light.

In the second state, after the expiration of the last breath, the deceased experiences secondary lights of five colors, arranged into *mandalas* or archetypal circular patterns. These lights correspond to the Buddha's "enjoyment body" (*sambhoga-kaya*). Again the deceased is exhorted to focus on and merge with the Clear Light or to use the unusual clarity of this state to meditate in the customary fashion.

Finally, the third transitional state is marked by the manifestation of less intense light, corresponding to the Buddha's "manifestation body" (*nirmana-kaya*). Now the deceased becomes aware of the life he or she has left behind, and is subject to all kinds of karmic illusions and fears. It is more difficult for him or her to concentrate on the spiritual process, but the *Bardo Thödol's* instruction continues to be read for the deceased.

In all three phases, the experiencing subject is capable

of receiving the wisdom teaching that allows him or her to penetrate the mystery of the human mind and attain liberation. However, it is a popular misconception that simply reading the *Bardo Thödol* to a newly deceased person can effect his or her liberation. In spiritual life, the result is always directly proportionate to individual effort. Thus whether deceased individuals will heed the instructions read to them depends almost entirely on whether they bring to their afterlife a sound commitment to, and ability for, self-transcendence.

SEE ALSO The Three Bodies of the Buddha

THE THREE TYPES OF KARMA IN HINDUISM

Ever since the 1960s, *karma* has been a buzz word in certain circles. It is widely used in the sense of "destiny" or "fate," and this corresponds to the popular understanding among Hindus and Buddhists. However, upon closer examination the notion of karma is rather more sophisticated.

This teaching goes back to the earliest period of Hinduism and is prominently featured in the *Upanishads*, which are esoteric scriptures building upon the Vedic revelation. Karma—the word denotes simply "action" in Sanskrit—was meant to explain the mechanism by which an individual undergoes repeated incarnations.

Karma is thought to work as follows: Every action, be it physical or mental, has its corresponding reaction. Thus, every intention, every thought, leaves an imprint in the subconscious, which then combines with similar imprints to form powerful traits (called *vasanas,* "scents"). These countless imprints are known as *samskaras,* which literally means "activators." As this designation suggests, the imprints are not mere passive deposits in the sub-conscious mind but are highly dynamic forces, which constantly agitate the mind. Their dynamics can readily be seen when we try to sit completely still and silence our thoughts.

The innate restlessness of the mind is responsible for our desires, which in turn prompt us to act, and our intentions and actions then feed back into the subconscious. Thus the action–reaction cycle is kept going indefinitely. Significantly, according to the Indian sages, the subconscious impressions remain intact after the death of the physical body. They are said to be responsible for the next incarnation, when the human psyche assumes a new body to continue its experiences in the material world. The subconscious impressions are also referred to as "karmic deposits" (*karma-ashaya*), and their results in life are called "karmic fruit" (*karma-phala*), or destiny. Often both aspects are simply called "karma."

There are three principal types of karma. First, there is karma awaiting fruition (known as *sancita-karma*) in the form of the karmic deposits in the subconscious; karma that has come to fruition in the present embodiment (called *prarabdha-karma*); and karma that is produced through our intentions and actions in this lifetime and that will come to fruition in a future existence (which is known as *vartamana-karma*).

Is there then no escape from the law of action and reaction? The Indian sages give us an optimistic answer to this question: The karmic wheel can be stopped, providing we eliminate the root cause of karmic conditioning, which is spiritual ignorance. We must realize the great Being, the atman or brahman, that is prior to the laws of space and time, including the moral law of karma. This optimism lies at the core of all the many spiritual paths of the East.

THE THREE KINDS OF SUFFERING
IN BUDDHISM AND HINDUISM

"Suffering," preached the German mystic Meister Eckhart in the thirteenth century, "is the swiftest steed carrying us to God." Byron had a similar intent when he wrote, "Sorrow is knowledge," for it is the trials and tribulations that ripen us. They are, as Shakespeare knew, heaven-sent.

Life affords us ample opportunity to experience sorrow. Indeed, "everything is sorrowful" (*sarvam duhkham*), as noted by Patanjali, the master who compiled the *Yoga-Sutra*. He merely echoed an insight expressed centuries before him by Gautama the Buddha. In the Buddhist tradition, suffering is listed as one of the three characteristics of conditioned existence. The recognition that human life is inherently limited and bounded by the inevitability of death is the starting point of many spiritual teachings, including Yoga, Vedanta, Samkhya, Buddhism, and Jainism. But rather than be intimidated by this fact, the spiritual traditions encourage us to overcome all sorrow or suffering.

According to the Samkhya school of thought, suffering is of three kinds: intrapsychic (*adhyatmika*), external or environmental (*adhibhautika*), and supernatural (*adhidaivika*). We are familiar with the first two types of suffering. In the case of intrapsychic suffering, the source of our misery lies within our own psyche: our impulses and desires, fears and misconceptions. External suffering, as the term indicates, arises from the outside world, such as pain caused by a wound. But what about the third kind?

The Hindu metaphysicians believe that we are subject to the influence of the stars and all kinds of invisible entities, the most dramatic form of influence being demonic possession.

As a species we have found all kinds of ways of dealing with suffering. Denial is one way; distraction is another. However, the only way in which we can prevent future suffering is through true wisdom, which reveals our essential identity to us. That identity is the transcendental Self (purusha), which is eternally untainted by pain, sorrow, frustration, and suffering. When we realize the Self, we simultaneously transcend suffering.

SEE ALSO The Three Characteristics of Conditioned Existence in Buddhism; The Four Noble Truths of Buddhism

THE THREE GEMS OF JAINISM

Jainism is the spiritual tradition founded by Mahavira, a contemporary of the Buddha, though its roots go much farther back in time, beyond the sixth century B.C. According to the *Tattvartha-Adhigama-Sutra,* the following three fundamental practices constitute the Jaina path of liberation: right view (*samyag-darshana*), right knowledge (*samyag-jnana*), and right conduct (*samyak-caritra*). These are known as the "three gems" (*ratna-traya*).

Right view is the basis for the other two. We must first have the right outlook on life before we can acquire deeper knowledge and adopt an appropriate course of action. Of course, right view presupposes a degree of spiritual understanding and sensitivity. The three practices are really interdependent. Thus the Jaina path has been compared to a ladder, with right view and right knowledge being the side poles of the ladder, and right conduct being the rungs leading up to the apex of spiritual liberation.

THE THREE REFUGES OF BUDDHISM

Ever since the days of Gautama the Buddha, men and women who were moved to join the Buddhist tradition have been solemnly repeating the following formula:

> I take refuge to the Buddha.
> I take refuge to the Dharma (i.e, the teaching).
> I take refuge to the Sangha (i.e., the spiritual community).

The Buddha, the Dharma, and the Sangha are also known as the "three gems" (*tri-ratna*). The Buddha is not only venerated as the founder of the Buddhist tradition but also as the supreme ideal of the perfected being. In certain schools of Mahayana Buddhism, the Buddha is even given the status of the ultimate Reality itself.

The Buddha's teaching is considered a source of unending inspiration. More than that, anchored as it is in Gautama's own spiritual struggle and final enlightenment, his teaching is a tool of empowerment for those who desire to follow in his footsteps.

The spiritual community, the third refuge or treasure, creates a supportive environment for the Buddhist monk or layperson—a constant reminder of the moral and spiritual values he or she has chosen to uphold.

The spiritual significance of teacher, teaching, and community is recognized in most spiritual traditions. Together, they serve as a solid foundation for inner work.

SEE ALSO The Noble Eightfold Path of the Buddha

~4~

THE FOUR COVENANTS IN JUDAISM

In both Judaism and Christianity, the notion of covenant between God and humankind is prominent. The idea was obviously adopted from the arena of political life. Thus the Hebrews were fond of forging alliances with other peoples, and these alliances were formalized in binding pacts, such as Abraham's agreement with the Amorites or Joshua's agreement with the Gibeonites. Judaism knows of four such solemn agreements, or covenants (*berit*).

The first covenant was made with Noah, Hebrew patriarch and survivor of the deluge. God had instructed him to construct a huge ark, which Noah (the name means "rest") faithfully did to the merriment of his neighbors. He, his wife, and three sons survived the inundation when it covered the earth for 150 days. When the water receded, the ark grounded on top of Mount Ararat. Even as Noah and his family offered their prayers of thanks, God caused a rainbow in the sky as a visible sign of his covenant that the earth would never again be destroyed by water.

God entered a second covenant with Abraham, another great patriarch. Scholars have fixed Abraham's date to the twenty-first century B.C. One day, according to Genesis (chapter 17), God commanded the ninety-nine-year-old Abraham, who was then still called Abram, to walk before him and be perfect. God gave him his new name and made a covenant with him and his descendants, telling him that his offspring would multiply immensely and that he would give him the land of Canaan forever.

What God demanded in return was that every male be circumcised. According to Genesis, Abraham lived up to the agreement and, despite his advanced age, did not exclude himself from this sacred operation. He and his wife Sarah, who was then ninety years old, begat a son—Isaac. This particular covenant is known in Hebrew as *berit milah* or "covenant of circumcision."

A third covenant was made with Moses on Mount Sinai. Moses, who may have been Egyptian by birth, is remembered as the prophetic "founder" of Judaism and was easily the most influential of Hebrew leaders. Apparently about 1,300 B.C., he freed the Hebrews from slavery in Egypt and led them to the Land of Promise, though he himself died before reaching Canaan, the "land where milk and honey flow."

According to the Jewish tradition, Moses received the ten commandments engraved on two stone tablets directly from God who appeared to him in a thick cloud enveloping Mount Sinai. The commandments are at the heart of Mosaic law.

The covenant made on that occasion was that God would work miracles and drive out the peoples inhabiting Canaan so that the Hebrews could move onto the land they had been promised by the Lord. In return, he expected the Hebrews to observe a variety of rituals stipulated by him and above all, worship him alone.

A fourth covenant was made with King David, a son of Jesse and father of Solomon. David lived in the tenth century B.C. and achieved fame for his inspired religious music and poetry, being credited with the authorship of the Psalms. God commanded him to rule with justice over Israel, so that he might gain victory over his enemies. David conquered Jerusalem for the Hebrews and established it as the holy seat of Judaism. Even the Christian community accepted the claim that the messiah would be born in David's lineage.

On the model of Judaism, the early Christians also availed themselves of the metaphor of covenant. They felt that Jesus' gospel represented a new covenant, replacing the old Mosaic covenant. According to Christian interpretation, the agreement God made with Abraham was a promise that was made law at the time of Moses but that found its true fulfillment in the teaching of Jesus.

A covenant implies that its terms are binding only so long as all of them are observed. The divine covenants are entirely crafted by the will of God, and are unilateral. While individuals have the choice of accepting or rejecting the covenant, they cannot alter its conditions. Acceptance implies blessings from on high, whereas rejection or violation brings condemnation and punishment in their wake.

THE FOUR NOBLE TRUTHS OF BUDDHISM

After his awakening under the *bodhi* tree more than 2,500 years ago, Gautama the Buddha resolved to share his newly won wisdom with other beings. In his very first sermon he summarized his understanding of life by preaching the four noble truths to a small group of ascetics who had come to hear him.

The first noble truth is that all finite things are shot through with suffering (*duhkha*). Every possible human experience contains an element of suffering. This is true even of the experience of pleasure or joy, for whenever we feel pleasure there is simultaneously, at the back of our minds, an awareness that the experience will not last and also that others may feel still greater pleasure.

The second noble truth concerns the cause of all suffering, which is our innate craving, or "thirst" for life and experiences. It is this craving that is at the root of the endless cycle of rebirths, or reincarnations, which keeps us fettered to finite existence. Closely associated with craving as the source of all our ills is spiritual ignorance, which blinds us to the true nature of existence.

The third noble truth is that craving, though without beginning, can end. We have the possibility of interrupting the vicious cycle of ignorance and experience, rebirth and suffering. And the way to extirpating all craving within us is the noble eightfold path of the Buddha, which is the fourth noble truth.

Those who follow the eightfold path are promised an end to all craving, ignorance, suffering, and limited existence, and the realization of *nirvana*. The Sanskrit word "nirvana" means literally "extinction" and refers to the extinction of desire and ignorance and their fatal consequences. However, the Buddhist scriptures do not merely delineate this ultimate goal of the Buddhist path in negative terms, but they also characterize nirvana as the condition of enlightenment in which there is peace, happiness, truth, wholeness, and deathlessness. In other words, contrary to some interpreters, nirvana is not just a nihilistic state, which would make little sense, but a positive state of freedom and perfection.

THE FOUR GOALS OF LIFE IN HINDUISM

According to Hinduism, there are four grand ideals or values that a person can pursue: the *purusha-arthas* or "human purposes." At the bottom of the scale is material welfare, which includes money, possessions, physical health, as well as power over others. Closely associated with these values is the pursuit of pleasure, whether sexual gratification, the appreciation of beauty, or the enjoyment derived from intellectual activity. Most people invest considerable energy in the pursuit of these first two "purposes."

In addition, there are two higher types of values. The first is moral integrity. A few exceptional individuals make this their principal objective in life, and in some cases, their exemplary lives include a passionate concern for the moral upliftment of their fellow beings through social activism. The highest value is embodied in the ideal of spiritual liberation. In Sanskrit, the these four goals are respectively known as *artha* (literally "thing"), *kama* ("desire"), *dharma* ("virtue"), and *moksha* ("liberation").

Spiritual liberation, or freedom, is what Abraham Maslow, the father of humanistic psychology, would call a profound "metavalue." Liberation stands for the realization of our innermost nature, the transcendental essence, or *atman* of Vedanta and Yoga. We can equate it with Self-realization, which is a very specific form of what Maslow called "self-actualization."

Through Self-realization we are freed from our own psychic conditioning and become open to the play of life as it unfolds spontaneously. Moksha is considered the highest human value because it integrates all others. Upon liberation, or enlightenment, we truly appreciate the three

values of material welfare, physical, emotional, and intellectual pleasure, as well as a moral way of life. We appreciate these values without being rigidly defined by them.
Through our inner freedom, we are able to fully appreciate
the place of material things, beauty, knowledge, virtue,
and even power in the scheme of things.

THE FOUR REFUGES IN JAINISM

Jainism, which is older than Buddhism, has an ancient
formula known as the "four refuges" (*catuh-sharana*),
which forms an integral part of the daily prayers and
affirmations of the pious Jaina. It runs as follows:

> I take refuge in the four:
> I take refuge in the *arahats;*
> I take refuge in the *siddhas;*
> I take refuge in the *sadhus.*
> I take refuge in the teaching taught by the *kevalin.*

The arahats are "worthy" practitioners of Jainism,
the blessed ones who attained enlightenment and im-
parted enlightenment to others. The siddhas or "accomplished ones" are the adepts who rose to great spiritual
heights by virtue of their steadfast application of the
moral principles embodied in the Jaina scriptures. The
sadhus are the venerable teachers and preceptors. Lastly,
the title *kevali* or *kevalin* refers to the liberated master
Vardhamana Mahavira himself, the last of the great pro-
mulgators of the Jaina tradition.

This formula is based on the belief that great masters,
even when they are no longer in the physical body, can be
sources of help for those who turn to them with an open

heart. Essentially the same practice can be found in other traditions. Thus Buddhist practitioners turn to the original Buddha, other Buddhas (whether transcendental or living), as well as human teachers for assistance on the spiritual path. In certain branches of Christianity, the pious address their prayers not only to God but also to Jesus, Mary, and a host of other saints.

THE FOUR STEPS TO GOD IN SUFISM

Sufism, the mystical tradition within Islam, recognizes four stages of spiritual ascent. The first stage deals with moral life, as codified in the *shari'ah*. The shari'ah is the canonical law of Islam, as revealed in the Koran and the *sunnah* (the spoken word and exemplary behavior of Muhammad) and elaborated by the theologians of the various Islamic schools.

The second stage is that of the *tariqa,* the mystical path, which is deemed "narrow" by comparison with the "wide" path of the shari'ah. Islamic esotericism (called *tasawwuf*) comprises many such distinct paths. The oldest path is that of the Qadiriyyah, founded by the celebrated Baghdad saint 'Abd al-Qadir al-Jilani in the twelfth century. This path, or mystical lineage, is found in many countries with a Muslim presence—from India to Morocco.

The third stage relates to the transcendental reality (*haqiqa*). This reality, or truth, is also called the "kernel" (*lubb*), after the Koranic phrase "those who possess the kernels," meaning those who have grasped the essential message of Muhammad's teaching. According to an old Sufi adage, one must break the shell in order to get to the kernel, which is to say, one must break with exotericism in order to enjoy the wisdom of esotericism.

The fourth and final stage concerns *ma'rifa,* or true knowledge, which is the mystical realization of the Divine. This idea corresponds to the Sanskrit notion of *jnana* and the idea of *gnosis* in the Gnostic tradition. In the Sufi literature, this "knowledge" is often mentioned together with *makhafah* (fear of God) and *mahabbah* (love).

The four stages have been interpreted as an upward journey, from the human world to the angelic realm (*malakut*), then to the level of divine power (*jabarut*), and finally to the dimension of divinity (*lahut*) itself.

THE FOUR LEVELS OF EXISTENCE ACCORDING TO THE KABBALAH

According to the Jewish mystical tradition, existence comprises four levels. The first level is *atziluth,* the world of emanation, which contains the ten *sefiroth* of the Kabbalah. Even though this is a most rarefied state of existence, it is nevertheless separated from the One (the *ain sof*) by many veils. Kabbalists picture a vast empty space between God, the One, and the universe with its four levels. It is God's pure will, in the form of light, that crosses the empty space and gives rise to the universe. That luminous link, issuing from God, is the world of *Adam Kadmon,* the Primordial Human, who is often regarded as a fifth level of existence. The level of atziluth, which is the most subtle state of creative potency, serves as a blueprint for the lower levels of existence.

The second level in the four-level scheme is *beriyah,* the world of manifestation. Here the creative potentiality of the ten archetypal principles (the sefiroth) is translated into actual reality in the form of harmoniously organized subtle energy.

The third level is *yetzirah,* the world of formation, which comprises the next-lower category of subtle forms.

Finally, the fourth level is *asiyah,* the world of visible things that are the most stepped-down version of the unmanifest archetypes within atziluth. If one compares the highest level of existence to a translucent vessel that presents barely any restriction to the light within and surrounding it, the other levels are progressively more opaque. At the level of the visible world of matter, the vessel's walls are so thick that they are impermeable to the divine light. Yet, because of the vessel's hollow interior, it is still capable of receiving the light. In fact, unlike atziluth which both receives and reflects the divine light, the shadow world in which we live is only able to receive—a humbling insight.

THE FOUR STAGES OF LIFE IN HINDUISM

Hinduism, like certain other traditions, sees life as a school. We are born into this world to learn certain lessons so that we may mature to the point where we discover our higher, spiritual destiny. Given this point of view, it makes sense to consider life as an unfolding of developmental stages.

Ever since the time of the *Upanishads,* the earliest of which date back to at least 1000 B.C., the Hindu authorities have spoken of four stages of life, called *ashramas.* The first twenty-one years are covered by the stage of the student, or *brahmacarya,* which literally means "brahmic conduct." Here the young individual is gradually introduced to the value system of Hinduism, being given a thorough grounding in the knowledge and wisdom revealed by the great sages and visionaries. This is a period of learning and chastity. The Hindu sages regarded sexual abstinence as crucial to the assimilation of higher knowledge. Even married adults were expected to practice sexual economy, because orgasm was considered wasteful of the body's life energy.

The second stage of life, extending from the twenty-second to the forty-second year, was known as *garhasthya*. This is the stage of the householder (*grihastha*), who is married, has children, earns a living, and assumes all the usual family responsibilities. In other words, the obligation during this phase is to simply be a useful member of society, all the while basing one's actions, feelings, and thoughts on the foundations laid during the brahmacarya stage.

The third stage of life begins, ideally, during the forty-third year, when, as the scriptures say, one's hair is starting to turn gray and one's children are grown up. This is the time to retire from the world, to enter the stage of the "forest-dweller" (*vanaprasthya*). The *vanaprasthya*, or hermit stage of life, is the beginning of renunciation. This meant so much more than retirement in our modern society. The forest-dwelling hermit was expected to cultivate solitude and resume the earlier studies of the sacred lore. If a man was married he would usually enter this phase together with his wife. He might have students of his own to pass on the wisdom as well as to help him with the daily chores of living. He was not merely doing nothing or pursuing hobbies. Rather, the vanaprasthya stage was understood as a period of intense study, contemplation, and giving up attachment to life.

Finally, the last stage is that of complete renunciation or *samnyasa*. At this point, the forest-dweller voluntarily abandoned even his meager livelihood and religious duties as a hermit in favor of the life of a wandering mendicant (*samnyasin*). From now on he had no home and no belongings (other than the clothes on his body, a begging bowl, and a staff). Like a bird, he moved freely about in the world, always trusting and contemplating the Divine in the hope of attaining release (moksha) from the endless cycle of repeated births and deaths. He had no further social obligations.

Ideally, the samnyasa stage began with the eighty-fifth year. However, in practice, the four stages were often collapsed into much shorter periods of time, and in not a few cases the householder stage was altogether bypassed, depending on a person's spiritual maturity and calling.

THE FOUR REQUIREMENTS FOR
PRACTICING VEDANTA

Vedanta is the most prominent metaphysical branch of Hinduism and comprises many schools. All of them are based on the sacred revelation of the *Vedas,* the four ancient collections of hymns, which were composed by the Vedic seers or *rishis.*

The study of the spiritual teachings of Vedanta was considered a great privilege, because it effectively placed in one's hands the key to true wisdom and enlightenment. The masters of Vedanta were therefore careful to impart their teachings only to those who were genuinely qualified to receive them.

According to Sadananda Yogendra's *Vedanta-Sara* ("Essence of Vedanta"), a popular Sanskrit manual belonging to the fifteenth century A.D., students of Vedanta must have a basic understanding of the Vedic tradition and be inwardly pure. More specifically, they must meet the following four requirements:

1. They must be able to distinguish between the eternal and the finite, which is a particular kind of sensitivity or intelligence;

2. They must be willing and able to renounce all desire for reward. In other words, they must demonstrate a considerable degree of unselfishness;

3. They must possess the "six means," namely tranquillity, restraint, renunciation, forebearance, concentration, and faith;

4. They must have an overwhelming longing for liberation, or enlightenment, which is the ultimate goal of Vedanta. Without such a deeply felt impulse toward liberation, students are unlikely to endure the hardships and tests of spiritual discipline or conquer the fickle mind, which constantly seeks pleasurable experiences rather than the truth.

It is clear from this that pupilage in the Hindu tradition, as indeed in any other spiritual tradition, is not merely an intellectual undertaking but an arduous path of self-transformation and self-transcendence.

THE FOUR STAGES OF BUDDHIST MEDITATION

Buddhism has a sophisticated culture of meditation (*dhyana*), and the Buddha himself was an accomplished and passionate meditator. It was through the process of meditation that he gained his enlightenment, after discarding all other means, notably the fierce asceticism he had pursued previously. He distinguished four levels of meditative realization connected with certain forms (*rupa*). The Pali texts call these levels *jhanas*, meaning "meditative absorption."

In the first meditation, all sensual desires are suspended and the space of consciousness is filled with joy and bliss born of detachment. In this state of one-pointed concentration there are still spontaneously arising thoughts, which are not, however, experienced as an obstruction.

When these thoughts or forms of awareness in relation to the object of meditation are also suspended, the practitioner enters the second level of jhana. Now only one-pointedness, joy, and bliss characterize the meditative state. Typical objects of meditation on this level are love, compassion, and sympathy.

On the third level of meditative absorption, the experience of joy is absent, and only bliss and one-pointedness are present.

On the fourth level, even the element of bliss has disappeared, and there is only a pervasive sense of equanimity or serenity in the midst of intense concentration.

These meditations are not an end in themselves. Rather they are the ladder upon which the Buddhist practitioner ascends to the final realization of nirvana.

THE FOUR LEVELS OF FORMLESS
REALIZATION IN BUDDHISM

Beyond the experiences of the four types of form-dependent meditation, as outlined above, Gautama the Buddha also taught four higher meditations giving one access to formless realms of existence. These are known as *arupa-jhanas,* or "meditative absorptions without form." They are as follows:

In the first formless absorption, the practitioner experiences infinite space. In the second, he experiences infinite consciousness. In the third, there is awareness of nothing-ness. The fourth and highest jhana consists in a conscious state where there is neither perception nor the absence of perception. This last realization is extremely subtle and can only be grasped intellectually in paradoxical terms. However, even this advanced state is not identical with nirvana.

What these meditations have in common is that the practitioner is completely shut off from the outside world and cannot be interrupted by any external stimulus. Rather, he or she will come out of the meditative state at a predetermined time or as a result of an inner impulse to re-enter conscious reality.

It is impossible to understand what these meditative realizations stand for apart from direct experience. The inner world is infinitely varied, and all kinds of categorizations are possible. For the Buddhist, this particular cartography of meditative states is merely intended to provide a pathway to the ultimate realization of nirvana. It is easy to get sidetracked into states that are less than nirvana and to confuse them with the final destination. All such models are meant to serve as roadmaps for the intrepid psychonaut who desires liberation, or enlightenment.

THE FOUR UNIVERSAL FEELINGS
ACCORDING TO BUDDHISM

The Buddhist tradition knows of four mental states that can be deliberately cultivated as meditation practices: friendliness (*maitri*), compassion (*karuna*), joy (*mudita*), and equanimity (*upeksha*). These are known as the four "brahmic" or "divine abidings" (*brahma-vihara*), also often referred to as the four "infinitudes" because their respective feelings must be radiated in all directions without qualification.

Thus in generating the mood of friendliness the spiritual aspirant must extend his feeling of good will to all beings, desiring for them the same benign existence that he might desire for himself. *Maitri* (or *metta* in Pali) is often translated as "love" but is more accurately understood to be friendliness or kindness.

The moral challenge implied in this practice is to look upon all others as "friends" (*mitra*) rather than enemies. So long as we see ourselves surrounded by enemies we remain defensive and closed. However, when we cease to take the behavior of others as a personal insult and, instead of contracting around our ego, remain in a friendly disposition, we make a positive contribution to the world. Not only do we lessen our own suffering, but, because of our nonreactive disposition, we also defuse tension and reduce conflict in the outside world. Thus we give others the opportunity to discover the virtue of friendliness and the advantage of happiness.

The practice of compassion likewise reduces the distance between us and others. By radiating compassion to all beings, human and nonhuman, the aspirant acknowledges his kinship with them. Since suffering is omnipresent, there is no lack of opportunity to be compassionate. By identifying with the suffering of others, the aspirant cultivates the desire to help them and lessen their burden.

The next practice is to expand one's inner joy to all others. Instead of identifying with the suffering of others, the aspirant learns to identify with their joy. This practice uses the contemplation of the moments of happiness experienced by others as the basis for wishing everyone unlimited good fortune and delight. Even though the spiritual aspirant understands that most people delight in rather ephemeral things, he nonetheless rejoices with them. He is able to do so wholeheartedly precisely because of his own nonattachment to the material world.

The final practice is to radiate equanimity, which is a kind of serene unconcern arising from a mind that has been thoroughly purified and is as stable as a mountain. The spiritual foundation of this virtue is the deep insight that, in the final analysis, all beings are the same. In Buddhist terms, this means that all beings are ultimately "void" or "empty," and that all the differences that separate us from one another make finally no difference at all.

Each of the four virtues is thought to have a close and a distant enemy. The distant enemy of friendliness, for instance, is ill will whereas the close enemy is lust. Thus the practice of friendliness involves the effort to prevent this feeling from degenerating into mere sensual desire or attachment. The distant enemy of compassion is cruelty. The close enemy is wallowing in the dark mood of pity. The distant enemy of joy is unhappiness. The close enemy is immersion into mere pleasure. The distant enemy of equanimity is agitation. The close enemy is cold indifference.

In Mahayana Buddhism, the four brahmic abidings are included among the perfect virtues of the *bodhisattva,* and they are thought to lead to rebirth in the heavenly realm of Brahma. As the name *brahma-vihara* suggests, these meditation practices very probably originated within Hinduism where they are mentioned, for example, in the *Yoga-Sutra* of Patanjali.

THE FOUR STATES OF CONSCIOUSNESS IN HINDUISM

According to Vedanta metaphysics, unqualified or un-differentiated awareness or consciousness (*cit*) is the ultimate Reality. Ordinary consciousness (*citta*) is merely a distortion or a lower manifestation of that absolute intelligence. The Vedanta authorities speak of four states (*avastha*) of consciousness.

The lowest state or level is deep sleep (*sushupti*) in which there is no awareness of external or internal phenomena, but which is nonetheless not completely devoid of awareness, because upon waking we can tell whether we have slept well. During deep sleep, the subject is thought to be a mass of unified consciousness and to experience the bliss of the absolute Consciousness. However, because self-consciousness is dismantled in the process of deep sleep, there is no continuity of awareness. In other words, deep sleep is automatic and unconscious Self- or God-realization.

The next level of consciousness is dream sleep (*svapna*), which includes a rudimentary form of self-awareness and awareness of inner reality. In this state we assume all kinds of roles and enact a great variety of dramas. With a little training we can remember our dreams quite well and may even become able to influence our dream life.

The third state is the full waking consciousness (*jagrat*), which is based on a well-defined sense of self. In this condition we feel that we are immaterial subjects inhabiting physical bodies in a dense material world. However, in regard to the fourth state of consciousness, which is Consciousness in its pure condition, even the ordinary waking state is like a dream.

The "Fourth," which is called *caturtha* or *turiya* in Sanskrit, is the transcendental Self itself. It is not the same as self-conscious awareness of external or internal phenomena, nor is it identical with unconsciousness. The Self is supraconscious and beyond ego, thought, feeling, and sensation. It is nondual, permanent, and continuous. Realizing it is deemed the ultimate purpose of human life.

Upon Self-realization, there is perfect continuity of awareness in all states of consciousness. Thus the Self-realized adept may be seen to sleep deeply, but upon waking he can remember all that has transpired around him. When tested at the Menninger Clinic, the modern yogi Swami Rama, founder of the Himalayan Yoga Institute in Pennsylvania, could produce at will the brain waves characteristic of deep sleep. Yet, after emerging from this state he could remember what had occurred during that period far more accurately than the experimenters themselves, who were supposedly in full possession of consciousness.

THE FOUR LAST THINGS IN CHRISTIANITY

Christian theology includes the study of the last things (*eschata*)—eschatology—namely death, judgment, heaven, and hell. Some denominations add the second coming of the Christ as a fifth *eschaton*. In other words, eschatology deals with the events at the end of individual life on the one hand, and the fulfillment of the collective destiny of humankind on the other.

The original Christian community believed that the "end of time" was near and that the "last days" had been inaugurated by the event of Pentecost, when the Holy Spirit descended upon the twelve disciples of Jesus. It was thought that a great upheaval was imminent, marked by the return of the Christ and the resurrection of the dead followed by God's judgment.

The apocalyptic mood of the early Christian community was shared by many others within the Judaic tradition. Ever since the eighth century B.C., the Hebrew prophets preached that in the future Yahweh would intervene in the world's affairs and judge not only Israel but all of humanity. That time of judgment, known as the "Day of the Lord," was understood to be a time of destruction as well as renewal in which Yahweh would triumph over evil.

By the second century B.C., this prophetic movement within Judaism had become apocalypticism—the teaching that on Judgment Day, in the words of prophet Daniel, those "who sleep in the dust of earth shall awake" and either be granted everlasting blessed life or be condemned to an eternal existence of torment and terror. This belief represented a major departure within Judaism.

The "reign of God" was thought to be inaugurated by a special messenger of God, the Messiah (the "anointed one"). The Hebrew community was eagerly anticipating his coming. At the beginning of the Christian era, several Jews claimed that status for themselves, including Jesus of Nazareth.

The early Christians took Jesus' crucifixion to signal the beginning of the end of time. Especially St. Paul argued that the death and resurrection of Jesus ushered in a new era moving humanity inexorably closer to Judgment Day. For him, the transformed Jesus—the Christ—was the first of many who would be thus glorified.

Jesus apparently taught that the kingdom of God was "at hand," which some of his followers interpreted to mean that Judgment Day was imminent. Two thousand years later, a similar apocalyptic mood still prevails in certain Christian sects, notably the Jehovah's Witnesses and the Seventh-Day Adventists. However, many Christians today prefer a metaphoric interpretation, which does not foresee a future cataclysm coinciding with the "second coming" but which understands the kingdom of God as an ever-present possibility for the individual: a spiritual rebirth in which the faithful discovers the omnipresent Divine in his or her heart and life.

THE FOUR WORLD AGES IN HINDUISM

In contrast to the modern conception of time, as an arrow pointing to the future, the Hindus have since ancient times operated with a cyclical notion of time. World ages follow one upon the other with a clear trend toward progressive moral and spiritual degeneracy, until the whole cycle starts anew—*ad infinitum.*

Like most other ancient traditions, Hinduism embraces the idea that in the remote past humanity lived in a "golden age" and that the present age is one of spiritual decline. The four world ages are as follows:

1. *Satya-yuga* ("age of truth"), lasting 4,000 divine years, during which humanity lived in perfect peace and harmony with Nature—a time when the sages and mystics were respected and when everyone had personal access to the higher dimensions of reality. People lived long and healthy lives. They were beautiful, strong, of great vitality, and giant size.

2. *Treta-yuga* ("thrice-lucky age"), lasting 3,000 divine years, during which humankind's moral purity was diminished by a fourth, as was people's strength, vitality, size, and length of life.

3. *Dvapara-yuga* ("twice-lucky age"), lasting 2,000 divine years, during which spirituality and morality were only half as strong as during the golden age, leading to a corresponding decrease in health, beauty, vitality, and so on.

4. *Kali-yuga* ("dark age"), lasting 1,000 divine years, during which spirituality and morality are at an all-time low, and which is marked by a preponderance of sin, sorrow, and ill health.

With the exception of the golden age of truth, the other world ages are named after throws of the dice, a favorite game in ancient India. *Kali* represents the unlucky throw.

In between these four eons (*yuga*) are periods of "dawn" and "dusk" lasting 800, 600, 400, and 200 divine years respectively. Thus the four ages and their respective periods of phasing in and phasing out comprise a total of 12,000 divine years, corresponding to 4,320,000 years according to human reckoning. The set of four ages is known as a "great age" (*maha-yuga*). One thousand such great ages are called a *kalpa,* and they make up a day in the life of the creator deity (Brahma). Evidently, the Hindus think in terms of vast cycles of time in which the material universe is destroyed and recreated over and over again.

According to Hindu chronology, present-day humanity finds itself in one of the dark ages, which is thought to have commenced with the death of the God-man Krishna after the great war related in the *Mahabharata* epic. His ascension to heaven is said to have occurred on February 18, 3102 B.C., which means that the troubling *kali-yuga* has barely begun.

THE FOUR SUNS IN THE
NATIVE AMERICAN TRADITION

According to the Hopi tradition, there have been four "suns," or cycles of creation. The people of the first world, called *tokpela* (endless space), lived in balance, harmony, and perfect well-being. They enjoyed purity and happiness. When their civilization began to corrupt, the Creator arranged a big cleansing.

Before unleashing the powers of Nature, the Creator instructed the faithful followers of the spiritual path to leave their homes and follow a certain cloud during the day and a certain star at night. They were all guided to a place of safety—a giant ant hill, the entrance to the world of the Ant People. The Creator told them to learn from the Ant People, who were industrious and cooperative and obedient to the plan of Creation.

In their underground hideout, the First People survived the holocaust. Everyone else perished in the ensuing volcanic eruptions.

The survivors of this worldwide conflagration repopulated the earth during the time of the second world, known as *tokpa* (dark midnight). Having learned from their stay with the Ant People, they busied themselves with building homes and trails and became creative artisans. But moral and spiritual corruption set in when they discovered trading, bartering, and hoarding goods, which led to quarrels and wars.

This time the Creator cleansed the earth by ordering the protecting spirits of the North and South Poles to temporarily leave their positions, so that the planet would spin free. The resulting pole shift caused great winds, and a huge ice sheet covered the earth.

After this second cleansing, the Creator blocked the soft spot at the crown of the head (the fontanelle), making it much more difficult to acquire sacred wisdom.

The survivors of the second world formed the seed population of the third, known as *kuskurza*. They grew quickly in numbers, and soon big cities were scattered all over the planet. In the course of building such a vast civilization, many people again forgot to sing the Creator's praise.

This time destruction came in the form of a huge flood. The virtuous people, who had been sealed off in hollow reeds by Spider Woman, survived the inundation. However, they had to travel for a long time before finding land, and even then were doomed to arduous overland migrations. The Hopi followed the Blue Star Kachina to their homeland.

According to Hopi prophecies, the same Blue Star Kachina will return and dance in the sky, as an omen that the destruction of the fourth world, called *tuwaqachi* (World Complete), was near. On August 7, 1970, hundreds of Hopis and white brothers witnessed a strange dancing light in the sky over Prescott, Arizona. Hopi traditionalists believe that this curious incident fulfilled the prophecy and that, therefore, we must now reckon with the imminent destruction of the fourth world, our own.

THE FOUR CARDINAL DIRECTIONS
IN VARIOUS TRADITIONS

In all traditional cosmographies, the four directions hold special significance. They mark sacred space, the Earth. The numeral four is generally given the symbolic value of stability, a characteristic of the Earth, which is often symbolized as a square.

The four points of the compass are widely associated with sunrise (East), sunset (West), noon (North), midnight (South). They also are related to the two equinoxes and the two solstices. In this way, the four directions are more than mere spatial reference points; they also tie in with the unfolding of time, as captured in the movement of the sun.

According to the worldview of the ancient Maya of Mesoamerica, each direction has a special deity, tree, bird, and color associated with it. Similar to Atlas, the four deities—called Bacabs—were giant beings holding up the pillars of the sky. They survived the great flood at the end of the last world age and were represented as old men. They were closely associated with bees and were considered actors who could disguise themselves as opossums. The Maya also thought that the Bacabs exercised a great influence on a year's fortune or misfortune, and it is not surprising that important rituals were associated with them. Some accounts replace these deities with giant trees that serve the same purpose of upholding the celestial vault.

East, the birthplace of the sun, was thought to be connected with the color red. West, the sun's grave, was given the color black. North, the direction associated with the pole star, was white, whereas South, the "great side of the sun," was yellow.

The Aztecs connected the four cardinal directions with particular phases of human life: East with youth, South with adulthood, West with old age, and North with death.

The North American Indian traditions have similar

ideas about the four cardinal points, associating them with specific spirit beings or "guardians" whom they invoked for protection before every ceremony. According to the Chippewa, the East is called Wabun, has the eagle as its totem, and is associated with spring and the color yellow. The spirit keeper of the South is Shawnodese, whose totem is the coyote. This quarter of the earth is connected with summer and the color green. The guardian of the West is Mudjekeewis who presides over autumn and sunset. The totem is the bear and the associated color is blue. The spirit keeper of the North is Waboose, whose totem is the white buffalo. The season connected with this direction is winter and the representative color is white.

Corresponding ideas can be found in the mytho-geographies of ancient Europe, the Middle East, India, and the Far East. In addition to the four directions, which effectively cover the horizontal plane, many traditions mention two more. These additional directions relate to the vertical axis, one going up (toward heaven) and the other going down (toward hell). Others, like the Hopi Indians, recognize eight directions, which include the four semi-cardinal points on the compass.

THE FOUR MATERIAL ELEMENTS
IN VARIOUS TRADITIONS

The idea that the material cosmos is an aggregate of four fundamental elements—fire, air, water, and earth—dates back to a hoary past. Barbara Walker's *The Woman's Dictionary of Symbols and Sacred Objects* offers the following ingenious explanation for the origin of this archaic notion: "The real origin of the elements lay somewhere in the

Neolithic Age, when people discovered that there are only four possible ways to dispose of their dead (other than cannibalism): burial, cremation, sinking in waters, or exposure to carrion birds of the air." Although we will never know for sure how our ancestors came to discover the four elements, it is clear from the world's cosmologies that this teaching was widespread in the ancient world.

Our Western notion of material elements derives from the cosmological speculations of the Greeks, notably the natural philosopher, poet, and miracle-worker Empedocles. He was born in the early fifth century in Acragas (the modern Agrigento) on the Mediterranean island of Sicily. For him, the four elements explained why there is change in the world. For, under the influence of the two cosmic powers—love and strife—the elements attract and repel one another, thus creating a wide variety of combinations.

Empedocles, moreover, believed that the qualities of color, heat, and moisture directly adhere to the indestructible elements. He failed to solve the problem of how permanent elements could possess apparently impermanent qualities. This difficulty later led Democritus to distinguish between primary and secondary qualities. It was also Democritus who appears to have invented the idea of atoms, ultimately indivisible fragments of those elements.

Plato and his pupils adopted Empedocles' teaching, which was probably strongly influenced by Pythagoreanism. But he and his fellow academicians gave it a new mathematical twist: They associated the four elements or basic substances with four fundamental geometric shapes— the tetrahedron, cube, octahedron, and icosahedron.

Long before the Greeks turned their attention to cosmological matters, the intellectual elite of India probed for answers to basic philosophical questions. Thus we find in the pre-Buddhist *Aitareya-Upanishad,* one of the earliest scriptures of the upanishadic genre, speculations about the four elements (*bhuta*) of nature. Subsequent schools within Hinduism often add a fifth element—ether or space (*akasha*) to this set.

While for the Greek philosophers the theory of the four material elements was primarily intended to explain the physical cosmos (or macrocosm), the Hindus extended it also to psychological phenomena (microcosm). Thus in the model of the seven *cakras,* or psychospiritual vortexes of the human body-mind, the four elements are assigned to the first four cakras in ascending order, proceeding from earth to water to fire to air. The purpose of this psychocosmological schema was not to provide food for idle curiosity but to give the spiritual practitioner a map for his or her inward journey. The underlying idea is that in order to realize the transcendental Self, one must go beyond the elements of Nature—completely transcend the body and the mind.

SEE ALSO The Five Elements in Chinese Metaphysics

~5~

THE FIVE DIVINE PRESENCES IN ISLAM

Under the influence of Neoplatonism, Muslim thinkers elaborated a metaphysical schema according to which reality exists on five levels. These are commonly known as the five divine presences or, collectively, as the synthesis of presences. Abu Talib, who lived in the tenth century A.D., provided a systematic treatment of them. They are as follows:

First is the Godhead (*hahut*), the ultimate Essence from which nothing can be taken away and to which nothing can be added, because it is all-inclusive. It is the Absolute which necessarily contains its own negation or self-limitation, thus being the source of the world's creation. Although the world appears to be other than the Godhead, it is nevertheless existing in and dependent on the Divine. The name *hahut* is derived from *huwa*, meaning "He," and referring to Allah, who, as the Koran states, is "all high" and "all glorious."

The second divine presence is the personal God, corresponding to the Christian "Father" and the Hindu "Lord" (*ishvara*). In Arabic, this level of existence is called *lahut,* a derivative of *al-ilah,* or "divinity." It is this personal God who can be referred to both as "the Compassionate" and "the Avenger," because this super-being includes countless qualities. He creates the world, gives and takes life, hears prayers, and forgives or punishes transgressions. Whereas the Godhead, which is inherently beautiful and merciful, is perfectly uniform, the personal deity entails a process of polarization into activity and receptivity. On the human level, this primordial polarity is mirrored in the distinction between male and female.

The third divine presence is the realm of power (*'alam al-jabarut*) inhabited by the archangels who surround God's "throne." This is also the domain of the higher paradises of the hereafter, but the ultimate paradise, the "garden of the essence," is the absolute Reality itself.

The fourth divine presence is the realm of dominion (*'alam al-malakut*), which is the world of the spirits (*jinn*), comprising both the lower paradises and the hellish regions.

The fifth divine presence is the material world, called *nasut,* which is farthest removed from the Godhead but which is still a manifestation of it.

THE FIVE AGGREGATES IN BUDDHISM

Gautama the Buddha taught that the human personality is composed of five fundamental constituents, known as the *skandhas* ("heaps"), or aggregates. They are in constant flux, and because of their impermanence do not provide a source of true happiness. The five aggregates are:

1. Form (*rupa*), which is the physical aspect of the personality;

2. sensation (*vedana*), which comprises all pleasant, unpleasant, or indifferent sensations arising from contact with the sensory world;

3. perception (*samjna*), which refers to all mentally assimilated sensations;

4. subliminal "activator" (*samskara*), which comprises all mental phenomena: dispositions and tendencies but also moods and ideas;

5. consciousness (*vijnana*), or awareness, which is the basis of the other four aggregates.

This teaching is intended to undermine the common belief that there is a continuous self (*atman*) that holds the various aspects of the personality together. Whatever sense of identity one may have, according to Buddhism it is necessarily an illusory identity deriving from spiritual ignorance. The sense of "my" or "mine" is equally false. In place of a stable self, there is only the continual modification of the five aggregates. The aggregates themselves are "without self" (*anatman*) or "empty" (*shunya*), and filled with suffering.

SEE ALSO The Twelve Links of Dependent Origination in Theravada Buddhism

THE FIVE CAUSES OF BONDAGE IN JAINISM

The unenlightened state is widely characterized as one of bondage, because we are not in touch with our true nature, which is inherently free. This idea is also crucial to Jaina metaphysics and its path of salvation. The *Tattvartha-Sutra,* a manual of the second century A.D., lists five causes of human bondage: erroneous views, lack of restraint, carelessness, passion, and activity.

1. Erroneous views (*mithya-darshana*)—which are also collectively referred to as errors (*pratyaya*)—comprises the following five components:

First, the habit of looking at reality, which has countless aspects, only from a single point of view—known as *ekanta* (literally "one-end"). Thus, the belief that the human being is mortal takes only the body into account but fails to consider the spirit, and vice versa. This kind of exclusivism tends to create dogmas that bind rather than liberate us.

Second, erroneous beliefs (*viparita*). One classical commentator singles out the belief that animal sacrifices lead to heaven as a case in point. The Jainas have always had a great reverence for all forms of life. They abhor violence, including violence done in the name of religion.

Third, doubt (*samshaya*), which makes us indecisive and thus disempowers us. Here doubt stands especially for the kind of self-destructive skepticism that prevents a person from moving along on the spiritual path, or from embarking on it altogether.

Fourth, the indiscriminate adoption of religious or spiritual disciplines called *vinaya*. Since spiritual life demands a wholehearted commitment, we need to carefully examine our options before we leap into anything. There is no benefit in making a career out of religious conversion, jumping from one tradition to another. We merely get confused and discouraged.

Fifth, misconception (*ajnana*), which is responsible for our mistaking right and wrong. It is considered to be either inborn or the result of misinformation. According to the Jaina tradition, there are 363 kinds of false assumption that can lead a person astray. Jainism offers itself as a path out of this thicket of possible misconception. Knowledge is power inasmuch as it liberates us from ourselves, our limited and warped views of reality.

2. The second major cause of bondage is lack of restraint (*avirati*). It is said to be of twelve kinds, since immoderate use can be made of the five senses and the mind and also since there can be a lack of compassion for the six classes of embodied beings (plants, animals, humans, etc.).

3. Another principal cause of bondage is carelessness (*pramada*), which is described as having fifteen varieties, namely gossip; idle talk about food, women, and politics; as well as carelessness about the five senses, passion, affection, and sleep.

4. A further source of human bondage and misery is passion (*kashaya*), which comprises anger, pride, deceitfulness, and greed—well known from other traditions.

5. The final cause of bondage is activity (*yoga*), which has a very special meaning in Jainism. According to Jaina philosophy, there are an infinite number of spirits (*jiva*). These have three main qualities—infinite awareness, bliss, and energy. In the unenlightened state, these qualities are blocked or obscured to varying degrees. The blockage of the spirit's infinite energy causes a certain type of movement or activity, which is called *yoga*. It is responsible for the intake of karmic "matter" on the part of the

spirit, which then leads to repeated births and deaths—the whole cycle of reincarnation, which binds the spirit to the world.

Only the "dry" spirit, free from passion and attachment, remains unaffected by the karmic matter. Karmic matter can adhere only to a spirit that is impure, or "moistened" by its own desires. The liberated being is motionless. At first, he or she still performs spontaneously those activities (like eating and drinking) that characterize the embodied state. But, at the instant of physical death, even these minimal activities cease, and the liberated spirit is entirely free from all karmic entanglement, living on eternally in perfect awareness and bliss and endowed with an infinite resource of energy.

THE FIVE BUDDHIST PRECEPTS

A Buddhist is someone who takes threefold refuge in the Buddha, the Dharma (teaching), and the Sangha (community), and who endeavors to observe the five precepts (*panca-shila* in Sanskrit, *pansil* in abbreviated Pali). These rules are not to kill, steal, indulge in sensuality, lie, or become intoxicated by liquor or drugs. These form a minimal moral code and are to be observed by monastics and lay followers alike. They are similar to the moral restraints (*yama*) of the eightfold yogic path taught by Patanjali and also have much in common with the ten commandments in Judaism and Christianity. In a way, they can be said to represent the quintessential requirements of a universal morality.

Buddhist monks and nuns are expected to adhere to five additional precepts, namely not to eat solid food after noon, attend worldly entertainments, use perfume or wear ornaments, sleep in a soft bed, and possess money or other valuables.

These precepts are not so much commandments as guidelines for sound spiritual living, which are formally or informally espoused. *Shila* is one of the constituents of the noble eightfold path of the Buddha.

THE FIVE CONSTANTS IN CONFUCIANISM

Unlike his contemporary Lao-tzu, who was a mystic, K'ung-tzu (Confucius) was primarily a teacher of moral or virtuous conduct. He described the way of life characteristic of the "true gentleman" (*chün-tzu,* "duke's son"), who strives to follow the mandate of heaven (*t'ein*). However, while Confucius himself endeavored to submit patiently to the will of heaven by following the way of the ancient sages, he advised people to respect the deities but keep them at a distance.

Confucius taught that there are five cardinal virtues by which human behavior can be regulated in harmony (*ho*) with heaven:

1. *Jen,* or humaneness, which stands for love and reverence for one's fellow humans. This is considered to be the most important virtue characterizing the true gentleman. In his *Analects* (VI.28), Confucius states: "To apply one's own wishes and desires as a yardstick by which to judge one's behavior toward others is the true way of jen." The basis for jen is reverence (*hsiao*) for one's elders or superiors and obedience.

2. *Li,* or ritual, which stands for the following of the Chinese customs. Ritual played a very important role in

ancient China, and there were 300 major and 3,000 minor rituals that had to be mastered. They ranged from sacred rites to everyday good behavior. Confucius believed that if the true gentlemen follow the rituals punctiliously, the rest of the people would faithfully observe their own duties. Thus harmony would prevail in society.

3. *I,* or uprightness.

4. *Chih,* or wisdom.

5. *Hsin,* or faithfulness, which refers to the virtue of keeping promises and meeting one's commitments properly.

For Confucius, obeying the will of heaven and nobility of character were one and the same. Inner harmony is mirrored in outer harmony. Confucius's ideals were so high that, aged fifty, he himself confessed to not having met them. Nonetheless, his wisdom has helped shape the Chinese character in decisive ways.

THE FIVE PILLARS OF ISLAM

Islam is founded on five ritual practices, which are collectively known in Arabic as *'ibadat,* meaning "acts of service, worship." They are also commonly referred to as the five pillars (*arkan ad-din*). The first and most important pillar is *shahada* ("testimony"), which is the avowal of the basic Muslim creed that "there is no god but Allah" and that "Muhammad is the messenger of Allah." Whoever utters this confession with sincerity is deemed a Muslim. The shahada is formally recited during the five daily calls to prayer, as well as on other special occasions.

Prayer (*salat*), which is performed at dawn, noon, mid-afternoon, sunset, and evening, is the second pillar.

Preferably, Muslims pray together in a mosque, and the Friday mid-day prayer is stipulated to be in a formal congregation. The prayer involves many ritual elements, including bowings and prostrations in the direction of Mecca.

The third pillar is *zakat* ("integrity"), or alms, which Muslims are required to give at the end of the year to the poor and underprivileged. Alms-giving is thought to purify a person's wealth and also is regarded as a loan to God which he will repay double. Alms-giving is different from charity, which is not obligatory but recommended as a highly meritorious practice.

The fourth pillar is fasting (*sawm*), involving the abstinence from food, drink, smoking, and other bodily enjoyments from dawn until sunset during the entire ninth lunar month of Ramadan. Most Islamic countries uphold this canonical ritual, though frequently people consume a full meal before dawn and after the evening prayer. Islam allows for other voluntary fasts. Muhammad's contemporaries were so keen on fasting that finally he had to curb their enthusiasm, because they were growing physically weak. The mystics of Islam, the Sufis, have tended to observe fasting more strictly.

External fasting is thought to promote internal fasting, which is the discipline of restraining oneself from indulging in the ego's numerous passions until everything is fasted except for the presence of God.

The fifth pillar is a highly ritualized pilgrimage (*hajj*) to Mecca, which every healthy Muslim is expected to make at least once in his or her lifetime. The understanding is that in doing the pilgrimage no one must compromise his or her social responsibilities.

The focus of this ritual, which has pre-Islamic roots, is the Ka'bah ("cube"), the large cubic granite structure covered with a black cloth that stands in the center of the Grand Mosque in Mecca. It contains the black stone that, according to a traditional saying of the prophet, came down from heaven. It is of ovoid shape and about eleven inches wide and fifteen inches high. During the siege of Mecca in 683 A.D. the Ka'bah was set on fire and the heat of the burning wood cracked the black stone into three large pieces and several smaller fragments. The pieces are now held together by a silver band.

For the Muslims, the Ka'bah is the axis of the world. Traditional Islamic cosmology envisions seven invisible Ka'bahs directly above it, which are located in the seven heavens. At the top of this axial arrangement is the throne of Allah, which is circumambulated by high angels, just as the earthly Ka'bah is circumambulated by humans. The famous twelfth-century mystic Ibn 'Arabi taught that the Ka'bah represents Being itself. The black color symbolizes the emptiness of the Divine which only those can realize who divest themselves of all traces of the ego.

The Shi'ah Muslims have three additional obligatory duties: to pay one-fifth of their income to the religious head (*imam*), to exhort others to do good and abstain from evil, and to take part in holy war (*jihad*) when it is called for in defense of an Islamic nation.

THE FIVE TANTRIC "M'S"

The Hindu Tantric tradition has two major branches, the "right-handed path" (*dakshina-marga*) and the "left-handed path" (*vama-marga*). The latter seeks to awaken the psychospiritual energy (*kundalini*) dormant in the human body by means of unorthodox rituals, notably the infamous "circle worship" or *cakra-puja*. In this rite, an equal number of male and female initiates are guided by an adept and his female consort in esoteric practices. The participants look upon one another as God (Shiva) and Goddess (Shakti) respectively.

At the heart of this ceremonial gathering is the highly stylized ritual of the "five m's" (*panca-makara*). This curious appellation derives from the initial letter of the five "ingredients," which all begin with the phoneme *m* in Sanskrit. They are fish (*matsya*), meat (*mamsa*), parched grain (*mudra*), liquor (*mada*), and sexual intercourse (*maithuna*). The first four are considered aphrodisiacs and are consumed in sequence. The climax of the rite is the sexual union between male and female participants, whereby the woman sits astride the man. It is she who assumes an active role, while the male initiate is expected to be entirely passive, like Shiva.

Through the control of breath and mind, the practitioner is able to circumvent ejaculation. Instead, the buildup of psychosomatic energy resulting from intercourse is deployed to arouse the kundalini force at the base of the spine and to guide it upward along the spinal axis. The release of this energy into the topmost psychospiritual center (*cakra*) at the crown of the head, or rather, slightly above it, coincides with the ecstatic state. Instead of physical orgasm, the initiate experiences the unsurpassable bliss of ultimate nonduality.

SEE ALSO The Seven Psychospiritual Centers (Cakras) in Tantrism

THE FIVE AUSPICIOUS EVENTS IN JAINISM

In Jainism, the enlightened teachers are known as *tirthan-karas* ("ford-makers") or *jinas* ("victorious ones"). They are the lifeblood of the Jaina tradition, who by their teachings and very existence, renew the ancient message of their contemporaries.

These beings bring infinite blessings into the world, and every aspect of their life is sacred. Five transition points in the life of a tirthankara are held to be especially auspicious: his conception, birth, renunciation, attainment of omniscience, and final liberation.

Whenever the Jainas install a new tirthankara image in their temples, they perform a ceremony that celebrates the five auspicious events (*panca-kalyana*). The person sponsoring the ceremony takes the part of Indra, the king of gods, and his wife assumes the role of Indrani, Indra's celestial spouse. Other members of their family enact the role of the human parents. The image itself is treated as the infant tirthankara. The ceremony is very involved, extending over several days, and it covers the tirthankara's whole life and spiritual growth.

When the image has been duly installed, the fifth auspicious event—that of nirvana—is celebrated. Henceforth it is treated as an object of great veneration, and is deemed to be the physical vehicle for the spiritual essence of that particular tirthankara.

THE FIVE SACRED EMBLEMS IN SIKHISM

The Sikh religion, which is an offshoot of both Hinduism and Islam, was founded by Guru Nanak in the fifteenth century A.D. He was the first of ten teachers, or *gurus,* venerated by the Sikhs. Belief in the ten gurus and in the *Adi Granth* ("Original Book"), which is a collection of sacred writings compiled in 1604 A.D., is a defining characteristic of Sikhism.

The *Adi-Granth,* also known as the *Granth Sahib* ("Book of the Lord"), begins with the words, "By the guru's grace, worship the one God." Although God is formless and indefinable, he should nevertheless be made the pivot of all one's thoughts and actions. Guru Nanak disavowed asceticism and celibacy, teaching the gentle path of spontaneity (*sahaja*), achieved through gradual disciplining of the body and mind.

The tenth and last guru, Gobind Singh, was the founder of the Khalsa ("pure") sect. The male followers of this sect wear the following five obligatory emblems, which are called the "five k" (*panj kakkar*), because they all start with the letter *k* in Sant Bhasa, a Punjabi dialect:

1. *Kesh*—the unshorn hair and beard;
2. *Kanga*—a comb, which is stuck under the turban;
3. *Kada*—a steel bracelet;
4. *Kachh*—knee-length trousers;
5. *Kirpan*—a sword.

These emblems date back to the time when Gobind Singh initiated the five chosen followers who had consented to lay down their lives at his command. After baptizing them, he had himself baptized by this newly initiated elite, which is known as the "five beloved" (*panj piyare*).

THE FIVE BODILY SHEATHS IN HINDUISM

The archaic *Taittiriya-Upanishad,* an esoteric Sanskrit scripture belonging to the eighth or ninth century B.C., speaks of five sheaths (*kosha*). We can conceive of them as coverings or casings inhibiting the light of the transcendental Self, or Spirit. They can also be understood as templates or filters. This teaching, which appears to be based not so much on speculation as occult experience, was later adopted by most Vedanta schools.

The coarsest or densest casing is the physical body composed of the four material elements. It is known as the sheath made of food (*anna-maya-kosha*).

More subtle and interpenetrating but also somewhat exceeding the physical body is the sheath made of life force (*prana-maya-kosha*). The life force (*prana*) manifests in the body as breath, but is more than that. This corresponds to the "etheric double" of Theosophy.

Next in this hierarchy of filters comes the mental sheath (*mano-maya-kosha*), which is responsible for all the processing of the input received from the senses.

This is followed by the sheath composed of intelligence (*vijnana-maya-kosha*). Intelligence is a function of the higher mind, which in other Hindu schools is called *buddhi.* Here is the birthplace of true gnosis, or wisdom.

The most subtle sheath, or casing, is the sheath composed of bliss (*ananda-maya-kosha*). This is the final veil separating the individual from the Absolute. Yet, bliss is the very nature of the Absolute, and thus this particular sheath also affords the closest communion with Reality.

Each sheath represents a progressively higher field of reality and experience. Thus it is easy to see why initiates endeavor to shift their awareness and identity from the lower to the higher sheaths, until, at last, they awaken as the Self itself, free from all coverings.

As in the case of the five divine presences in Islamic metaphysics, the five sheaths are also regarded as manifestations of the Divine. However, the Divine—or the transcendental Self (atman)—is most evident when awareness is withdrawn from the lower casings and focused on the sheath of bliss. That ultimate covering is the most translucent. But the initiate is asked to rend asunder even that delightful veil and to *become* the Self, which is none other than the ultimate, suprapersonal foundation of all existence.

SEE ALSO The Four Material Elements in Various Traditions

THE FIVE SENSES IN VARIOUS TRADITIONS

"The senses lead to heaven or hell." This statement of the *Agni-Purana,* a Hindu religious encyclopedia, succinctly summarizes the traditional spiritual perspective on sensory perception. As this medieval scripture further explains, a person goes either to heaven or to hell, depending on whether the senses are restrained or active. So long as the senses are fully active, they draw our attention to the objective world. However, when they are checked, our consciousness turns inward, and it is within that we may find heaven.

When the Hindu texts speak of the five sensory "gates" (*dvara*), they mean the sense functions of seeing, hearing, smelling, tasting, and touching and their respective organs. These gates are the medium through which we experience the material or sensate world with its countless objects. The *Mahabharata* epic compares the senses to lamps placed on a high tree which illumine all things in proximity and which produce knowledge. However, the sages of India also understood that the knowledge derived from the senses is rather limited. Sensory perception is confined to the material realm and is excluded from all the subtle (*sukshma*) dimensions of the cosmos. Thus it can tell us nothing about the spirit world or the Divine.

In fact, according to all traditional teachings, sensory perception tends to cast a spell over us. This is poignantly expressed in the *Bhagavad-Gita,* the favorite spiritual book of the Hindus. As this work explains, when our attention flows out into the world through the senses, we are apt to become attached to material objects. This attachment inevitably gives rise to anger, because we can never hold on to anything. Anger is followed by bewilderment, and bewilderment mixes up our memory, so that we forget who we truly are, namely beings who are not dependent on any objects. Once our memory is confused, our innate wisdom is obscured, and we are quite lost.

The ethical teaching offered in the *Bhagavad-Gita* has an alternative to this fatal orientation: We may continue to move among the objects of the world but must do so with great self-discipline, without either feeling attached to them or repulsed by them. Only when we cultivate genuine serenity will our senses serve a benign purpose and not mislead us.

In the ordinary individual, lacking wisdom, the senses behave like unruly horses. The yogi, however, has learned to master them rather than be mastered by them. More than that, the accomplished initiate is capable of switching off the sensory functions altogether. This technique is known in Yoga as sense withdrawal (*pratyahara*), which is likened to a tortoise retracting its limbs.

The Buddhist scriptures speak of "guarding the senses" (*indriya-samvara*). This consists in not succumbing to the allurement of sensory input, either in general or in its details. This practice precedes meditation but is also to be applied at all other times, in which case the practitioner is promised unalloyed inner happiness.

In the *Tao Te Ching* (XII.1), the "old master" Lao-tzu observes that "the five colors blind a person's eyes; the five musical notes deafen a person's ears, and the five flavors ruin a person's taste buds." In other words, the onslaught of sensory input spoils and ultimately destroys the individual. In the *Chuang Tzu* (VII), a well-known Taoist scripture named after its author who lived in the fourth century B.C., this point is illustrated in the following allegory.

Long ago, Hun-tun ("Chaos"), who governed the center of the universe, hosted the emperors Shu ("Brief") and Hu ("Sudden"), who ruled over the South Sea and the North Sea respectively. Wondering how they might repay Hun-tun's hospitality, they said to each other: "All people have seven openings, so that they can see, hear, eat, and breathe. Poor Hun-tun has no openings at all. Let's repay his kindness by boring him some!" Every day they drilled another hole into him, and on the seventh day Hun-tun died.

Beyond its obvious cosmological significance, this allegory also can be applied in a psychological and spiritual context. The seven openings (two eyes, two ears, two nostrils, and one mouth) are the gateways by which a person's inner wholeness is interrupted, unless the openings are carefully guarded.

Some Hindu scriptures list five additional (conative)

sense organs, namely glottis (*vac,* "voice"), hands, feet, anus, and genitals. To this is frequently added, as an eleventh sense organ, the lower mind (*manas*). The lower mind is the rallying point for all sensory input and is carefully distinguished from the higher mind, or *buddhi,* which is the source of true knowledge.

Because of the great importance of the (lower) mind in the process of sensory perception, the Buddhists typically count it as a *sixth* organ of sense—in addition to eyes, ears, nose, tongue, and skin. As the *Dhammapada* (III.5), a popular Pali Buddhist scripture, states:

> Those who restrain the mind,
> which is far-ranging, roaming on its own,
> incorporeal, and hidden,
> are freed from the bonds of Mara [the Evil One].

THE FIVE ELEMENTS IN CHINESE METAPHYSICS

Just as the ancient Hindus and Greeks, as well as the medieval Christian philosophers, analyzed matter into four basic elements, so the Chinese cosmologists distinguished between five fundamental dispositions, or elements, of Nature. These five elements, called the "five movers" (*wu hsing*), are earth, water, fire, wood, and metal.

In the *White Tiger Discussion,* a Chinese work dating from the first century A.D., these five phases of Nature are correlated with other pentad sets, as follows:

WOOD	FIRE	EARTH	METAL	WATER
East	*South*	*Center*	*West*	*North*
Green	*Red*	*Yellow*	*White*	*Black*
Liver	*Heart*	*Spleen*	*Lungs*	*Kidneys*
Benevolence	*Ceremony*	*Trustworthiness*	*Righteousness*	*Wisdom*

Other correlations that can be made are:

WOOD	FIRE	EARTH	METAL	WATER
expansion	fusion	moderation	contraction	consolidation
movement	space	situation	form	time
wind	heat	humidity	dryness	coldness
sour	bitter	sweet	spicy	salty
emotive	sensitive	reflective	deductive	instinctive
anger	joy	thinking	sorrow	fear
eight	seven	five	nine	six

These correlations are made possible by the fundamental parallelism that exists between the macrocosm and the microcosm. In other words, the five constituent elements are not only found in the material cosmos but also in the human body-mind.

The five elements have their root in the incessant movement of Nature, which is governed by the dynamic between the *yin* (feminine) and the *yang* (masculine) principle of existence. In fact, the five elements constantly replace one another. Thus water quenches fire, fire melts metal, metal cuts wood, wood digs the earth or soil, and the earth dams water.

This patterned and cyclical understanding is crucial to Chinese medicine, which includes the healing of the human psyche. Health, or well-being, is understood as the ability to function fully and cooperatively within the continuously changing circumstances of the larger society and Nature.

According to some Chinese texts, this fivefold pattern was also important in regulating an emperor's life and government. The emperor was not merely a secular ruler but a spiritual being, on whose behavior depended the fate of the Chinese nation. He was expected to fulfill the law of heaven and thus to bring peace and prosperity to his subjects.

~ 6 ~

THE SIX DAYS OF CREATION IN THE
JUDEO–CHRISTIAN TRADITION

In the Judeo-Christian tradition, God is above all the creator of the world. Thus the Bible opens with the story of creation in six days, or seven days if God's day of rest is included. According to the biblical myth related in Genesis 1:1–31, on the first day God created light, causing the division between day and night. On the second day he created the firmament (heaven), separating it from the cosmic waters. On the third day he created land and sea and vegetation. On the fourth day he created the lights in the firmament. On the fifth day he brought forth the creatures of the ocean and the air. On the sixth day he created the land animals and, at the apex of the pyramid of creation, he fashioned the human being. Unlike the animals, he made the two original human beings, male and female, in his own image. He blessed them and ordered them to have dominion—modern authorities prefer to speak of stewardship—over the earth.

The creation narrative emphasizes that when God contemplated his creation, he deemed it good. On the seventh day he rested. This served as a model for the week of six working days and one day of repose, the *shabbat* or sabbath. When Moses brought down the inscribed stone tablets from Mount Sinai, the Israelites learned that the fourth of the ten commandments was to keep the seventh day holy to commemorate the corresponding time in God's creation. The Christian tradition echoes the Hebrew creation story when it has Jesus crucified in the sixth hour of the sixth day of the week. Since Jesus' resurrection occurred on a Sunday, Christians celebrate the sabbath on that day.

There is a second creation narrative in Genesis 2:4–3:24, which is considered the older version, dating back perhaps to the tenth century B.C. It includes the story of Adam and Eve.

THE SIX ANGELIC BEINGS IN ZOROASTRIANISM

Zoroaster (Zarathustra) taught that two ultimate principles—good and evil—are governing the universe. The good principle, which he called Ahura Mazda ("Wise Lord"), is surrounded and assisted by six immortal spiritual beings, the Amesha Spentas ("Immortal Holy Ones"). They appear to be personifications of virtues or existential qualities:

1. *Vohu Mano* ("Good Mind"), who appeared to Zoroaster in his forties and brought him before the throne of Ahura Mazda;
2. *Asha Vahista* ("Best Justice"), who is connected with fire as a symbol of purification;
3. *Khshathra Vairiya* ("Desired Sovereignty"), who has dominion especially over metal;

4. *Spenta Armaiti* ("Holy Surrender"), who is associated with the earth;

5. *Haurvatat* ("Perfection"), who presides over the plant kingdom;

6. *Ameretat* ("Immortality"), who rules the watery element.

To these is often added Ahura Mazda himself as their supreme leader. Sometimes Sraosha ("Obedience") takes his place. All are regarded as actual entities who can be, and are, invoked in prayers. The teaching of the Amesha Spentas has decisively influenced the Hebrew, Christian, and Muslim ideas about angels and demons.

SEE ALSO The Two Primordial Powers in Zoroastrianism

THE SIX SYSTEMS OF HINDU METAPHYSICS

Of all cultures of antiquity, India spawned the greatest diversity of philosophical thought. Its intellectual elite embraced an enormous spectrum of philosophical positions—from materialism to ritualism to lofty idealism. It gave rise to three great spiritual traditions, namely Hinduism, Buddhism, and Jainism, which all brought forth their own galaxy of sophisticated thinkers.

Within the fold of Hinduism, the following six classical systems of thought are traditionally distinguished: Mimamsa (speculative ritualism), Vedanta (nondualist metaphysics), Nyaya (logic), Vaisheshika (natural philosophy), Samkhya (enumerative metaphysics), and Yoga (mysticism). These are technically known as "view-points" (*darshana*). Each viewpoint, or system, has its own distinct schools, authorities, and literature.

The Mimamsa system is concerned with interpreting the age-old Vedic rituals and elaborating an ethical context for them. Its position is found codified in the *Mimamsa-Sutra* of Jaimini, composed around 200 B.C. The Mimamsa thinkers were primarily concerned with understanding the spiritual significance of *dharma,* or virtue. They taught that moral action, that is, action in keeping with the spiritual code of the Vedic revelation, improves the quality of one's life in the present and also secures a benign existence in the hereafter.

The Vedanta system, which consists of numerous schools, is based chiefly on an exposition of the *Upanishads,* the esoteric scriptures that are the concluding portion of the Vedic canon held in veneration by the pious Hindu to this day. Vedanta is spiritual metaphysics that interprets reality from a nondualistic perspective. According to this tradition, our ordinary consciousness gives us only a distorted view of existence, because it is anchored in a clear-cut division between subject and object. At a higher level of human development, or spiritual maturity, this separation of the perceiving subject from the perceived object is completely nullified. We then realize that the ultimate essence of all things is singular and that we are identical with it. This identity is epitomized in the classic Vedanta affirmation, "I am the Absolute" (*aham brahma asmi*) or "Thou art That" (*tat tvam asi*).

Vedanta metaphysics is inherently practical, for it endeavors to show us a way out of our ordinary consciousness and perception and to help us realize the transcendental Self (*atman*), which is none other than the transcendental Ground of the world, or *brahman*.

Vedanta was first codified in the *Brahma-Sutra,* authored by Badarayana about 200 A.D. This work, together with the principal *Upanishads* and the *Bhagavad-Gita,* is a cornerstone of Vedantic philosophy. Its terse and mostly incomprehensible aphorisms (*sutra*) have given rise to a large variety of interpretations, each crystallized into an autonomous school.

Nyaya, as codified in the *Nyaya-Sutra* of Gautama about 500 B.C., grew out of the tradition of philosophical debating. It is chiefly concerned with articulating the rules of logic and argumentation. In its metaphysical ideas it is close to the Yoga system.

The Vaisheshika ("distinctionism") system distinguishes the differences between things. Founded by Kanada about 500 B.C., it is an effort to understand such philosophical categories as substance, quality, the universal, and the particular. This system, which, like Nyaya, never won many followers, comes closest in intent to philosophy in the modern Western sense. Samkhya was founded by the sage Kapila, who is credited with the authorship of the *Samkhya-Sutra.* However, this work belongs to a relatively recent period, whereas Kapila appears to have lived as long ago as 600 B.C. The standard text for this system is Ishvara Krishna's *Samkhya-Karika,* composed around 350 A.D.

The Samkhya thinkers were predominantly interested in enumerating and describing the principal categories of existence. The classical school of Ishvara Krishna distinguishes twenty-four principles of existence. These are thought to account for the countless phenomena of Nature (*prakriti*). Beyond these forms are the innumerable spirits or transcendental Selves (*purusha*), which are pure awareness, forever witnessing the continuous motion of Nature.

Closely associated with the Samkhya system is Yoga, which was formalized by Patanjali in his *Yoga-Sutra*. No definite date is known for Patanjali, who has been placed as early as 500 B.C. and as late as 200 A.D. This system, also known as Classical Yoga, is a systematization of some of the fundamental ideas, beliefs, and practices of the Yoga tradition. Like Vedanta, the Yoga system has a practical and spiritual orientation. However, in contrast to Vedanta and in consonance with the other systems, Yoga teaches that there is not merely a single transcendental Self (atman), but countless such Selves (purusha). Later schools of Yoga favor a nondualist (Vedantic) interpretation of reality.

It is quite remarkable that these contrasting viewpoints all find accommodation within the Hindu tradition. They are considered "orthodox," even though some of their teachers firmly rejected the authority of the Vedic revelation, as did Gautama the Buddha. Today Vedanta is the most prominent and active philosophical position among Hindus who received a more traditional education. It also is a favored metaphysical system among Western students of Asia's spiritual heritage.

SEE ALSO The Twenty-Four Principles of Existence in Samkhya

THE SIX YOGAS OF THE BUDDHIST TEACHER NAROPA

The Kagyupa school of Tibetan (Vajrayana) Buddhism differentiates between two approaches to spiritual practice: the path of form and the formless path. The formless path, or *mahamudra* ("great seal") teaching, has been called

Tibet's version of Zen. It is founded on the realization of emptiness (*shunya*) and clarity.

The path of form consists essentially in the six yogas of Naropa. It is so called because in order to transcend the mind this approach employs specific practices that explore various aspects ("forms") of the human body-mind. Naropa is one of the most celebrated teachers of Mahayana Buddhism. He lived in Bengal in 1016–1100 A.D. and for eight years held the office of abbot at the famous Buddhist university of Nalanda. He resigned this prestigious position in order to enter into discipleship under Tilopa. The ardor of the pupilage is legendary. Naropa, in turn, was the teacher of Marpa, who taught Tibet's most beloved yogi-saint, Milarepa.

The six yogas of Naropa are:

1. The Yoga of Psychic Heat (*tumo*) consists in the generation of tremendous psychosomatic heat by means of breath control and intense visualization. This practice raises the temperature of the body to such a degree that accomplished practitioners can sit naked on the snowy mountain peaks of the Himalayas and even dry wet cloths wrapped around them. But the purpose of this exercise is not to demonstrate the body's extraordinary powers but to realize the ultimate bliss of enlightenment.

2. The Yoga of the Illusory Body (*gyulu*) aims at recognizing the illusory nature of the human body and of the world as a whole. At the core of this approach are meditation and visualization practices that give the yogi direct experiential confirmation of the fact that the body is a mental construct.

3. In the Yoga of the Dream State (*milam*) the adept learns to enter the dream state at will. Gradually he appreciates that the waking state is also dreamlike and can be manipulated so as to yield access to the ultimate Reality.

4. The Yoga of the Clear Light (*ösel*) consists of meditation techniques that bring about experiences of the white light seen after death, which is the doorway to the formless Void, or the pure awareness and bliss of enlightenment.

5. The Yoga of the In-Between State (*bardo*) is based on meditations through which the after-death realms, as described in the Tibetan Book of the Dead (*Bardo Thödol*), can be consciously accessed. The idea is that when one becomes acquainted with those realms prior to death, one does not get allured by them after the dropping of the body, but is able to focus on the Clear Light leading to liberation.

6. The Yoga of Consciousness Transference (*phowa*) consists in moving one's awareness outside the body. The favored exit point is the fontanelle at the crown of the head. When this technique is mastered, the adept then expects to be able to consciously leave the body at the moment of death and enter at will another form of his or her choice.

THE SIX DEGENERATIONS IN CONFUCIANISM

The *Analects* (XVII.8), which preserve the teaching of Confucius, contain a conversation between him and a certain Yu, who was ignorant of the sayings about the "six degenerations." Confucius explains them to him as follows (in Arthur Waley's rendering):

Love of goodness without love of learning degenerates into silliness. Love of wisdom without love of learning degenerates into utter lack of principle. Love of keeping promises without love of learning degenerates into villainy. Love of uprightness without love of learning degenerates into harshness. Love of courage without love of learning degenerates into mere recklessness.

The "true gentleman"—the ideal man in Confucianism—must be properly informed, or the virtues he pursues become mere caricatures of harmonious behavior. For instance, villainy may result from keeping a promise that is detrimental to the other person. Through learning (*hsüeh*), which is not simply book knowledge but assimilation of the wisdom of the ancients, all excesses can be avoided.

SEE ALSO The Five Constants in Confucianism

THE SIX VIRTUE PERFECTIONS IN MAHAYANA BUDDHISM

In contrast to Hinayana (Theravada) Buddhism, which is the path of the *arahat* ("venerable" monk), Mahayana Buddhism revolves around the ideal of the *bodhisattva* ("enlightenment being"). The bodhisattva strives toward enlightenment by practicing the six virtues to perfection. He or she vows to postpone entry into final liberation (*nirvana*) until *all* beings are awakened and saved. The six virtue perfections, or *paramitas,* are as follows:

1. The perfection of generosity (*dana*). The practice of this virtue consists of total beneficence. The bodhisattvas do not even seek to hoard personal merit, but give away everything for the moral and spiritual upliftment of others.

2. The perfection of discipline (*shila*). The bodhisattvas are fully committed to most rigorous discipline, not for any selfish reasons but to gain enlightenment and a favorable rebirth solely for the sake of others.

3. The perfection of patience (*kshanti*). The bodhisattvas are resolved to be infinitely patient and tolerant.

4. The perfection of exertion (*virya*). The bodhisattvas refuse to be diverted from their spiritual struggle, persisting in their effort to reach enlightenment even in the face of the greatest obstacles. They know that only when they are awakened can they serve the awakening of others.

5. The perfection of meditation (*dhyana*). The bodhisattvas understand that meditation is the single most important practice for penetrating the fog of conditioned existence and for seeing reality with clear eyes. In particular, they appreciate that meditation undermines the illusion of the ego-personality, which experiences itself as separate from all other beings. Meditation is thus the basis for empathetic and compassionate action.

6. The perfection of wisdom (*prajna*). The bodhisattvas know that without wisdom, their service to others would be of doubtful value. Without wisdom, they would be like the blind leading the blind. However, upon the dawning of true understanding, action becomes skillful and truly compassionate.

Sometimes the Mahayana scriptures add four more virtue perfections, namely right method, right resolve, power, and doctrinal knowledge. Here power (*bala*) stands for the ten powers of a *buddha,* an awakened being, which all relate to certain kinds of deep and instantaneous knowledge.

~ 7 ~

THE SEVEN AGES OF HUMANKIND
ACCORDING TO CHRISTIANITY

St. Augustine, who lived from 354 to 430 A.D., has been called the father of Christian theology. His model of the seven ages of humanity enjoyed great influence in medieval times.

According to the biblical creation story, God created the world in six days, resting and enjoying the fruit of his labors on the seventh. The Manichaean sect dismissed this myth on the grounds that it anthropomorphized God. It implied, they argued, that God had become fatigued from his creative efforts. St. Augustine, who was a convert from Manichaeanism, was eager to show that the Manichaean objection was based on a childish literal interpretation. He argued that God created the world all at once and that human culture is unfolding in seven phases.

According to St. Augustine, the first age, marking humanity's infancy, extends from Adam to Noah (covering ten generations). Humanity's childhood extends from Noah to Abraham (again ten generations). The period from Abraham to David (fourteen generations) represents the third age, of adolescence. The fourth age, of adulthood, covers the era from David to the captivity of the Jews in Babylon toward the end of the sixth century B.C. The fifth age, corresponding to early senescence, extends from the Babylonian exile to the coming of Jesus Christ. The sixth age, which is still in progress and which corresponds to late senescence, commenced with the mission of Jesus Christ. The seventh age, yet to come, ushers in the glorious kingdom of God. It has no end and therefore transcends history.

THE SEVEN PSYCHOSPIRITUAL CENTERS (CAKRAS) IN TANTRISM

Hindu esotericism, particularly Tantrism and Hatha Yoga, teaches that the material body is interpenetrated and surrounded by several bodies, or "sheaths," composed of subtle, energy-like matter visible only to clairvoyant sight. These bodies serve as templates for the physical body. Thus the nerve plexuses on the material level are energy vortices on the subtle planes.

Seven principal psychospiritual vortices, called *cakras* ("wheels"), are commonly mentioned in the esoteric literature. Sometimes spelled *chakras,* they are as follows:

1. The lowest vortex, corresponding to the sacro-coccygeal nerve plexus, is located at the base of the spine. It is known as the *muladhara-cakra,* which literally means "root-prop wheel." This is a very important psychospiritual center because it is the location of the dormant *kundalini* or coiled energy, the inlet, as it were, for the cosmic life force. In the ordinary person, that energy is in a

state of almost complete potency, and a mere trickle of that energy maintains the physical body.

2. The *svadhishthana-cakra,* or "self-standing wheel," is superimposed and related to the sacral plexus. A large amount of the body's dynamic energy is used up by this center, which governs the sexual drive and reproductive system. Hence most traditional schools emphasize the importance of celibacy, not for any prudish reasons but because orgasm consumes precious energy that could otherwise be helpful in one's spiritual transformation. The Japanese locate the *hara* at this plexus.

3. Known as the *manipura-cakra* or "jewelled city wheel," the third vortex is located at the navel. It corresponds to the solar plexus and is associated with the human will. Its activation can lead to out-of-body experiences and psychic powers, notably healing.

4. The *anahata-cakra* is in the center of the chest. The Sanskrit word *anahata* means "unstruck" and refers to the uncaused cosmic sound—*om*—that can be heard when attention is focused intently on this locus. This cakra, corresponding to the cardiac plexus, is considered to be the seat of feeling, especially that of love.

5. The *vishuddha-cakra* ("purified wheel") is located at the throat and corresponds to the pharyngeal plexus. It is responsible for speech but also, when fully activated, for enormous bodily strength.

6. The *ajna-cakra,* or "command wheel," is situated at the space between the eyebrows and corresponds to the pineal plexus. It is also widely referred to as the "third eye." This is the place where thought transference occurs,

and where the teacher contacts and guides the pupil tele-pathically.

7. The highest psychospiritual center of the body is the *sahasrara-cakra,* the "thousand-spoked wheel," corresponding to the ventricular plexus. This vortex is located at the crown of the head or, to be precise, slightly above the head. It is also known as the thousand-petaled lotus. The cakras are commonly depicted as lotus flowers with varying numbers of petals, and this particular vortex at the apex of the spinal axis looks to clairvoyant vision like a cascade of light filaments. This is where the human being is in contact with the Divine.

In Hatha Yoga and Tantrism in general, the serpent power, or *kundalini-shakti,* is conducted through all the cakras until it enters the thousand-spoked center at the crown of the head. When this occurs, the individual consciousness is drowned in untold bliss, merging with the primordial consciousness, or transcendental Awareness (*cit*).

Each cakra is thought to be a portal to a specific state of consciousness and reality, but only the topmost cakra gives one access to the Divine itself, or enlightenment. This is the ideal place for exiting the body consciously at the moment of death.

There are other models of the cakra system, some mentioning fewer, others many more, psychospiritual centers of the body. But the schema of seven vortices is particularly popular, perhaps because of its archetypal appeal, since in many traditions the number seven is associated with levels of reality ("heavens").

THE SEVEN HEAVENS IN VARIOUS TRADITIONS

The great cultures of antiquity understood the cosmos as a multilevel structure, with the earth occupying the midway point. Above the earth they conceived the abode of the gods, or beings of light, and below it the realm of the dead and demonic beings.

In ancient India, where the number seven occurs again and again in metaphysical thought, seven realms or zones (*loka*) were distinguished. Except for the lowest realm, these are occupied by gods and sages of various spiritual stature. In descending order, the seven lokas are:

1. *Satya-loka,* the "realm of truth," which is inhabited by four groups of deities who live for the entire life span of the cosmos.

2. *Tapo-loka,* the "world of asceticism," which is occupied by three groups of deities.

3. *Jana-loka,* the "world of people," which is inhabited by four groups of deities who have mastered the elements and the senses.

4. *Mahar-prajapatya-loka,* the *"mahar* world of the Creator," which is the realm of five groups of deities who have mastered the elements and live for a thousand world cycles (*kalpa*).

5. *Maha-indra-loka,* the "great realm of Indra," which is inhabited by six groups of deities who have acquired the eight great psychic powers of Yoga and who live for one full world cycle.

6. *Antariksha-loka,* the "realm of the mid-region," which is the habitat of the solar system and other stars.

7. *Bhu-loka,* the "earth realm," comprising the earth with its seven continents, seven nether regions, and seven hells.

Transcending these seven regions within the "cosmic egg" (*brahma-anda*) is the boundless and indescribable dimension of the Divine itself.

The ancient Mesopotamians believed in a sevenfold division of the underworld and may have entertained a similar notion with regard to heaven. The seven celestial realms were presumably associated with the seven planets known to humanity at that time.

Building on archaic Mesopotamian ideas, Muhammad, the founder of Islam, preached that there are seven heavens. The first heaven (closest to matter) is of purest silver, and it is here that Muhammad met Adam and Eve in his experience of paradise. The second heaven is like polished steel. Here the prophet of Islam found Noah. In the third heaven, which is studded with shining jewels, he met Azrael, the angel of death, who keeps track of all births and deaths. The fourth heaven, of finest silver, is the home of the angel of tears, who weeps unceasingly for the sins of humankind. The fifth heaven, of pure gold, has the avenging angel. Here Muhammad encountered Aaron. In the sixth heaven, the seat of the guardian angel of heaven and earth, he met Moses.

Only the seventh heaven, of unalloyed luminosity, is perfectly blissful. This highest spiritual realm is "the garden" (*al-jannah* in Arabic), or paradise. The Muslims think of paradise as a refreshing oasis, offering shade from the burning heat of the desert sun. In it flow abundant rivers of fresh, clear water, as well as rivers of nourishing milk, golden honey, and delicious wine. In the words of Muhammad, the faithful men will enjoy the company of "wide-eyed houris of the likeness of hidden pearls," who are virgins yet "chastely amorous."

In later periods, an eighth level was added to the celestial realms because the Muslim theologians thought there would be more saved than condemned souls. Beyond the seventh (or eighth) heaven, the spiritual realm that is most remote from the material universe, abides the great Beyond. In the gulf between the seventh heaven and the Beyond is what the Koran calls "the lote tree of the uppermost limit," which shades paradise. This realm will not be destroyed when the universe dissolves at the end of time.

According to Islam, just how remote that Divine is from its creation is borne out by the following tradition. Muhammad once asked the archangel Gabriel whether he had ever seen the Lord. Gabriel replied that there are 70,000 veils of light between him and Allah and that if he as much as approached the outermost veil he would be instantly consumed. Yet, Muhammad himself was granted the favor that was denied even to the highest angelic beings. As the Koran states, the prophet ascended in body and soul to paradise and from there to the Divine Presence itself—"a thing too stupendous for the tongue to describe or for the imagination to picture."

The notion of seven heavens is also prominent in early Jewish mysticism prior to the Kabbalah. Thus in the Heikhalot school, the seven heavens are known as the "divine palaces" (*heikhalot*), which the mystic in quest of God must traverse. Each heavenly domain opens its gates only to those who know the appropriate occult names of God and the associated secret signs.

THE SEVEN NETHER REGIONS
IN VARIOUS TRADITIONS

The Sumerian myth of Inanna's descent into the nether-world refers to seven gates. Goddess Inanna had to abandon one item of her gear at each gate, and thus entered the last gate completely naked and divested of all her divine powers (*me*). The Sumerian name for the underworld is *kur,* meaning "mountainous region." One reaches it by crossing the "river of death," heading downward. This is the place where all human souls have to go after the death of the physical body. Only the gods are destined to enjoy the elysium of heaven. It is a place of no return, as the Goddess Inanna discovered. Only because God Ea revived her, was she able to return to the bright regions of the living above the underworld. The Sumerian texts are not very precise about the topography of the underworld, but the mention of seven gates and the general downward direction of travel suggests seven levels.

This idea may have given rise to the notion of a similar hierarchy in the heavenly domain, as is the case in Islam, which incorporated many ancient Mesopotamian metaphysical elements.

At a still earlier time, the Indians developed a complex cosmography, which distinguishes seven nether regions (*patala*) and, below them, seven hells (*naraka*). Some Hindu authorities, such as Manu, speak of twenty-one hells, which are abysmal places of punishment for the wicked. In contrast to certain Christian teachings of eternal damnation, however, these hellish realms are not final destinations. Rather, they are transitional locations in which the soul finds itself as a consequence of earlier actions and intentions and where it can learn important lessons to create for itself a more benign destiny in future embodiments. The entire process is governed by the iron-law of karma.

THE SEVEN LIGHTS OF THE *ZOHAR*

Most spiritual traditions associate the Divine with light. Some schools equate the two, others make a careful distinction between them, making light inferior to God. Thus, Judaism holds that Yahweh created light, which must not be confused with physical light, since the sun was created only on the fourth day of creation. Since the light was the first emergent reality, it is considered a fit symbolic reminder of the presence of God in his creation.

It was from within a fiercely burning bush that God's voice called out to Moses, asking him to remove his shoes for he was standing on sacred ground. Moses shielded his eyes ("hid his face"), because he was afraid to look upon the Lord. Later, after Moses had delivered his people from the yoke of the pharaoh, God handed him tablets upon which he had engraved the ten commandments. On that occasion, the Lord appeared out of the cloud that had covered Mount Sinai for six days, and he looked like a devouring fire. No mortal, the Bible states, could ever behold the face of God.

For forty days and nights, Moses remained on the mountain receiving God's extensive instructions. Among other things, he was given detailed instructions for making a seven-branched candlestick (*menorah*) out of pure gold.

The Hebrews symbolized God's living presence—first in the tabernacle tent in the desert and later in the temple at Jerusalem—by the seven lights of the seven-branched candlestick that stood in front of the holy of holies. This ancient tradition is observed even today, for one or two menorahs are found in the sanctuary of every synagogue.

An esoteric explanation of the seven lights is found in the *Zohar*. The *Zohar* ("Splendor") is to Jewish mystics what the Old Testament is to Hebrew orthodoxy. This esoteric Aramaic commentary on the Pentateuch (the first five books of the Bible), which first appeared in the latter half of the thirteenth century, is the most influential work of the Kabbalah. Its influence extended to Christianity, since many Christian thinkers of the sixteenth and seventeenth century were fascinated with it as well. Traditionalists ascribe the *Zohar* to Simeon bar Yochai, who lived in Palestine in the second century A.D. and is said to have composed it while dwelling in solitude in a cave for thirteen years. However, most contemporary scholars see in it the compilation or creation of Moses de Léon, a great Kabbalist who lived between 1250 and 1305.

The *Zohar*, or Book of Splendor, speaks of seven lights within which dwells the "most ancient of the ancients," the *ain sof*. The seven lights are the seven great spirits who stand before God's throne—the spirits of life, sanctity, wisdom, eternal unfolding, truth, strength, and omnipotent love. These are associated with the colors of the spectrum: red, orange, yellow, green, blue, indigo, and purple.

THE SEVEN RITES IN THE NATIVE AMERICAN TRADITION

A sacrament is a ritual action that manifests the sacred. The Sioux, who call themselves Dakota ("Allied"), know of seven such sacraments or "sacred fireplaces." These were revealed by Black Elk (Hehaka Sapa), an Oglala Sioux sage, to a white man (Joseph Epes Brown) so that the heritage could be preserved. Black Elk, who died in 1950, received the sacred knowledge from Elk Head (Hehaka Pa) with the charge to hand it down. Brown's book *The Sacred Pipe* records his conversations with Black Elk on the seven rites.

Common to all the ceremonies is the smoking of the sacred pipe (*chanunpa*). It is believed to be instrumental to the survival of the Native Americans: Without the peace pipe and the spirituality for which it stands, the people are destined to perish. The pipe is the medicine man's most important implement. It is used to send prayers to the Great Spirit and other entities in the invisible realm. According to Sioux mythology, the sacred pipe was a gift from White Buffalo Cow Woman. The seven rites are as follows:

1. At least once in his life, though usually at puberty, the Plains Indian was encouraged to go on a *vision quest.* The Lakota word is *hanbleceya,* which means "crying for a vision." This expression captures the great trial the vision quest represents. This paramount ritual, lasting between two to four days, involves fasting (sometimes even abstention from water), chanting sacred songs, dancing, and prolonged prayer at an isolated spot in the wilderness. Through this ritual, the seeker hoped to contact the spirit realm and obtain guidance for his life.

2. The sun dance (*wiwanyag wachipi*) is the annual thanksgiving ceremony celebrated by all Plains Indians, which includes many rituals. Its purpose is to express gratitude to the Great Spirit and ask for strength and life for the Sioux Nation. This celebration of the renewal of life

is held on the day of the full moon in either June or July. Preceded by two days of ritual preparation, on the third day of the festivities the dancers had bone skewers inserted into their back muscles. Then they dragged heavy buffalo skins around until the skewers tore loose. On the fourth day, the dancers ran around the center pole of the lodge until they fainted from sheer exhaustion. At the final stage of the ritual, the dancers were fixed to the pole by ropes attached to skewers that had been inserted into their chest muscles. The dance was over when the flesh was torn and the blood offering had been made. The Sun Dance is still performed in a modified form by today's Plains Indians. Because of the large number of spectators, it is nowadays held outdoors.

3. The rite of the sweat lodge (*onikare*) is known as the "sweat" (*inipi*). The "sweat" is a sacred ritual of purification performed before ceremonies and the vision quest. The sweat lodge is a dome-shaped structure made from saplings and covered with hides or other material that keep out the light. The darkness is symbolic of the soul's ignorance. Inside the lodge, water is poured on heated rocks in the central altar to produce steam. The ritual can last several hours and is usually accompanied by prayers and songs.

4. A sacred rite known as the *ishna ta awi cha lowan* was performed after a girl's first menstruation. She was secluded in a specially built tent (*tipi*) where she underwent various purification rites and also received the medicine man's blessings. Henceforth she had to think of herself as Mother Earth.

5. The ceremony of "making of relatives" (*hunkapi*), which is said to go back to the time when the Sioux

made peace with the Ree (Arikara), is meant to extend the love for the Creator to his creatures. Originally a four-day ceremony, the hunkapi, which involves much exchange of gifts, is today celebrated primarily in the form of weddings.

6. The ceremony of the "throwing of the ball" (*tapa wanka yap*) was played by four teams. In the center of the court was a young girl. Her part in the play was to toss the ball (representing the universe) toward either of the four cardinal directions, while the adult players struggled to get the ball back to the center, the sacred location of Wakan Tanka.

7. The "keeping of the soul" ritual, which was prohibited by the American government in 1890, involved taking a lock of hair from the head of the recently deceased person and purifying it in the smoke of burning sweet grass and through prayers. The lock stood proxy for the soul. This rite had the purpose of purifying the soul of the dead so that he or she could become one with Wakan Tanka, the Great Spirit. The lock was wrapped in a buckskin and was safely kept in a protected corner in the tipi of the soul keeper. The rest of the body, properly bundled up, was placed on a scaffold in a tree away from the camp. Keepers of souls were not allowed to fight or hunt and had to live a holy life. The soul was released on an auspicious day in a separate complex ceremony.

THE SEVEN CAPITAL SINS IN CHRISTIANITY

Gregory the Great (c. 540–604 A.D.), the father of the medieval papacy who modestly described his own writings as "bran" in comparison with the "wheat" of St. Augustine's profound theological legacy, compiled a list of seven cardinal sins. This compilation achieved almost doctrinal status during the European Middle Ages. Dante used them as a framework for his vivid descriptions of purgatory in his *Divine Comedy.*

The seven sins, which are deemed to be at the root of all evil behavior, are pride, covetousness, lust, envy, gluttony, anger, and sloth.

In contrast to crime (which is a violation of civil law) and vice (which is a violation of the moral code of a society), sin is considered an offense against the Divine itself. Christian theologians distinguish between mortal (deadly) and venial sins. The former entail a fall from grace, estranging the sinner from God. The latter are less serious but nevertheless call for the sinner's repentance and submission to penitence. The seven cardinal sins are also often referred to as "deadly" or "mortal" sins, but this is incorrect, because they are not punishable by death. The biblical Greek word for sin is *hamartia,* meaning "missing the mark." Sin is a deviation from the will of God, or the spiritual path. In the final analysis, the sinner is always egocentric.

Pride is self-conceit as well as contempt for others. Covetousness is excessive desire for possessions, notably those of others. Lust is inordinate and inappropriate sexual desire, which leads to the abuse of one's own body and the bodies of others. Envy, in Thomas Aquinas' definition, is "sorrow for another's good." It is the nagging feeling of upset about another person's good fortune. It is often regarded as an outgrowth of pride. Gluttony is excessive desire for food and drink—a sin that Jesus himself was unjustly accused of. Its inclusion in the list of seven capital sins has sometimes been justified by the fact that gluttony can lead to worse sins.

Ever since the New Testament, the Christian tradition has viewed anger as a violent emotion that undermines reason and proper behavior, possibly leading to the commission of still more serious sins. Some modern theologians, especially those with a psychological and feminist orientation, have protested against the unqualified inclusion of anger among the seven capital sins. Today anger is widely regarded as a normal human emotion, which can have constructive effects, such as in social protest. The righteous anger of Jesus, who threw the money lenders out of the temple, is generally cited as an example of constructive anger. However, we must note that anger often manifests as petty selfish anger, which is certainly destructive.

Sloth is laziness that is self-centered and leads to isolation from others and from the Divine.

The negative attitudes behind the seven cardinal sins are recognized and condemned by all spiritual traditions. Mainstream Christianity differs from most other traditions in one important point: It views humanity as fundamentally sinful, having inherited its flawed character from Adam and Eve, the first sinners who turned away from God. This doctrine is mitigated by the correlative view that the death of Jesus on the cross reconciled humanity with God and that the spiritual discipleship of Jesus the Christ leads to the forgiveness of all sins.

THE SEVEN VIRTUES IN CHRISTIANITY

In his *Republic,* Plato recognized four cardinal virtues, namely prudence, justice, temperance, and fortitude. The Greeks called these virtues *arete* or "excellences" and sought to adhere to them as high philosophical ideals.

Their cultivation was thought to build good character and fortune.

These virtues were adopted by Christian theologians, who added faith, hope, and love (or charity). According to Catholic teaching, these three are said to be infused into the soul at the moment of baptism as gifts of the Holy Spirit.

St. Augustine defined prudence as "love that distinguishes with wisdom that which hinders it and that which fosters it." St. Thomas Aquinas considered it to be an intellectual virtue, which guides us in our choices, allowing us to see that which promotes our greatest well-being.

Justice is an attitude to life that endeavors to render to each being what he or she deserves. Christians have adopted the idea of a just or righteous God from the Hebrews and, like them, sought to model human behavior on this divine trait. In Christian ethics, emphasis is placed on the fact that for justice to be true it must be tempered by charity, or love.

Temperance is moderation in all things. This virtue is rooted in the idea common to all ancient cultures that the divine realm is inherently harmonious and that it is incumbent on humanity to likewise establish harmony on earth.

Fortitude, or courage, is resilient steadfastness in the face of life's adversities. Valued very highly throughout the ancient world, fortitude became a hallmark for the early Christians, who suffered greatly from persecution and martyrdom under the Roman empire.

Faith is explained as fundamental trust in, and loyalty to, God, Jesus Christ, or the Christian revelation. It is more than mere intellectual assent, or belief, but involves the whole person. As St. Paul preached, individuals are not saved by their works but by their faith. However, the distinction between faith and belief is often blurred in practice. Hence St. Anselm, the eleventh-century scholastic, was able to coin the famous Latin phrase *credo ut intelligam,* "I believe in order to understand."

Hope is a positive emotional disposition in which the individual desires that which is believed to be possible, such as forgiveness of sins, grace, and resurrection.

Love, or charity, is perhaps the most typically Christian of the seven virtues. It is that benevolent attitude by which we embrace others as if they were our brothers and sisters, with the intention of promoting their greatest well-being. This kind of love is understood to be fashioned after the love demonstrated by God toward his creation when he allowed his son, Jesus, to be crucified for the benefit of all humankind.

THE SEVEN CHRISTIAN SACRAMENTS

A sacrament is a significant rite or action that brings a person into the presence of the sacred reality. St. Augustine called it "the visible form of invisible grace." All religious traditions include sacraments, such as initiation and purification rites. In the twelfth century, Hugh of St. Victor listed thirty sacraments in his *De Sacramentis Christianae fidei* ("On the Sacraments of the Christian Faith"). Today Roman Catholicism, as well as the Eastern Orthodox Church and many Anglican churches, recognize the following seven:

1. Baptism is an initiation rite in which the individual (usually an infant) is either immersed in, or sprinkled

with, water to purify body, mind, and soul, and to die with Christ and to rise again with him. This ritual marks a new beginning, effecting a spiritual regeneration that incorporates the individual into the Mystical Body of Christ.

2. Confirmation is a ritual by which the individual, usually a young adolescent, is strengthened by the Spirit to fulfill the promises made on his or her behalf by spiritual representatives at the time of baptism.

3. The eucharist, also known as the Lord's Supper, is the principal sacramental rite of Christian worship. The word "eucharist" stems from the Greek *eucharistia,* meaning "thanksgiving." This rite remembers the meal celebrated by Jesus the evening before his crucifixion at which he consecrated himself as the true paschal lamb. At the core of the eucharist lies the ceremonial partaking of Jesus' blood (in the form of wine) and flesh (in the form of bread), which has been interpreted in many ways within the Christian community. Essentially the eucharist is a means of manifesting the presence of the risen Christ among the celebrants.

4. Penance is the acknowledgment and rejection of sin, sometimes before the congregation, based on a feeling of remorse and the willingness to make restitution followed by absolution. Penance is repentance, which may involve prayers, pilgrimages, retreats, or good works intended to reconcile the sinner with God or the Church.

5. The sacrament of unction entails anointing the sick with oil. This rite was formerly called "extreme unc-

tion," since it was granted only to those approaching death. Since Vatican II, the Catholic Church has regarded this sacrament as a part of its healing ministry. Anointing is frequently accompanied by petitionary prayer for the recovery of the sick person, as well as laying on of hands.

6. Holy orders refers to certain official roles within the Christian ministry. Thus the Eastern Orthodox and the Anglican Churches recognize the three major orders of bishop, priest, and deacon. The Roman Catholic Church added to these the subdeacon, which was abolished under Paul VI. The former duties of subdeacon are now fulfilled by lay readers and acolytes.

7. Matrimony, or marriage, is a covenant between a man and a woman. Since earliest times, Christians have viewed the human marriage bond as symbolic of the union between the Christ and the Church.

The sacraments, which are valued as channels of divine grace, continue to be subject to theological analysis and modification in light of the changing sociocultural conditions. However, their essential nature remains a *mysterion,* which is the Greek translation of the Latin term *sacramentum.*

THE SEVEN SACRED CAVES OF THE MAYA

According to the *Popul Vuh* ("Book of the People") of the Quiché Maya, when there was still darkness abroad in the world the original Maya lived in Vucub-Pec ("Seven

Caves"), Vucub-Zivan ("Seven Ravines"), or Tulan-Zuiva ("Tulan Cave"). Upon the coming of dawn, they crossed the ocean from east to west.

The Cakchiquel Maya remember their origins slightly differently. Their *Memorial Cakchiquel* states that the seven Maya tribes arrived at the Seven Caves from the west.

The Aztecs, the "people of the sun," likewise believed that they came from Chicomoztoc, meaning "Seven Caves," in their homeland of Aztlan.

Every year, the Hopi Indians remember their own crossing of the ocean by boat in the Flute Ceremony. Upon their arrival in America, they too lived in seven caves, and later named their seven original villages after these caverns.

Scholarship regards the Seven Caves as a primarily mythical place. Even the discovery, in the early 1970s, of seven caverns in the bedrock beneath the Pyramid of the Sun at Teotihuacan (near Mexico City) need not change this view. A similar seven-lobed cave was found under the High Priest's Grave temple in Chichen Itza. It could be reached through a shaft that was sealed with seven graves filled with all kinds of sacred objects. The ancient Maya generally had a great fondness for caves, which they experienced as places of spiritual power. Several deities have caves as their habitat.

In his book *Mexico Mystique,* Frank Waters suggests that we may regard the seven caves as a "universal myth." In support, he refers to a legend, current in the fifteenth century in Spain and Portugal. According to this story, in the year 734 A.D., seven Christian bishops escaped the Moorish conquest by sailing westward where they discovered the Island of the Seven Cities. It was this legend that prompted Coronado's unsuccessful search for the seven golden cities of Cibola.

A more striking parallel can be found in the Jewish tradition. Kabbalists speak of the seven chambers of the universe of Beriyah, which bear the following mysterious names: the holy of holies (*kodesh kedashim*), desire (*ratzon*), love (*ahavah*), merit (*zekhut*), luster (*nogah*), essence of heaven (*etzem hashamayim*), brickwork of sapphire (*livnat hasappir*).

In Frank Waters's view, the seven caves of the Maya are the seven psychospiritual centers (cakras) of the human body. This interpretation is indirectly supported by the seven caves under the Pyramid of the Sun at Teotihuacan. The four largest caves are arranged like the petals of a flower. The fifth forms a stem from which branch off the remaining two caves on either side. The cakras are often depicted as lotus flowers (*padma*) in Hinduism and Buddhism. In the archaic *Rig-Veda* (III.31), seven sages are said to have driven cattle out of a cave. It is clear from the context that this is to be understood in symbolic terms, for by recovering the cattle the sages discovered the "whole path to truth."

In his book *Secrets of Mayan Science/Religion,* Hunbatz Men, a contemporary Mayan shaman, mentions the seven powers of the human body–mind that allow the initiate to become one with God. According to him, they are represented on a stone tablet found in Aparicio, Veracruz, which depicts a human figure with seven serpents as its head. Hunbatz Men writes: "The Mayan masters teach that we are the integration of the seven powers of light, traveling in the form of the serpent, undulating eternally with movement and measure." He relates the seven powers to the seven cakras, thus making a fascinating connection between the Maya and the Indians.

THE SEVEN SAGES IN VARIOUS TRADITIONS

According to Sumerian/Akkadian mythology, there were seven sages who created early civilization, bringing much wisdom and knowledge to humankind. They are said to have sprung from the river with the task of ensuring that the plan of heaven is implemented on earth.

The Mesopotamian tradition remembers only four of the seven by name: Nunpiriggaldim, Piriggalnungal, Piriggalabzu, and Adapa. The last-mentioned is the best known. Berossus, a Babylonian priest of the third century B.C., identified him as Oannes.

Babylonian texts describe Adapa as having been created by God Ea. He was an exemplary man, serving the God as high priest at the temple in Eridu. He enjoyed fishing in a local lagoon. One day a sudden wind toppled his boat, and Adapa angrily cursed the spirits of the air, immobilizing them for seven days. Displeased with the sage, the great God Anu ordered him to ascend to heaven for judgment. Ea, wanting to protect her creation, advised the sage on how to impress Anu and the other Gods with the proper behavior. Indeed, he succeeded in appeasing Anu's wrath, and the God even offered the sage the water of life. Following Ea's warning about the offer, Adapa refused to partake of the divine draft, which would have made him equal to the Gods. Anu broke into uncontrollable laughter at the foolish refusal and promptly sent Adapa back to earth. It appears that all seven sages managed to incur the displeasure of the Gods in some way.

The tradition of the seven sages is also found in the *Rig-Veda,* the oldest literary document in the world. More and more scholars believe that some of the hymns of the *Rig-Veda* recollect an era preceding that of the Sumerian civilization. It is therefore quite possible that the Sumerian myth of the seven sages was derived from an earlier Indian version. There are many connections between Sumer and India, which still await a far-sighted explorer.

In India, the seven sages (*sapta-rishi*) are remembered as Atri, Gotama, Vaishtha, Vishvamitra, Jamadagni, Kanva, and Bharadvaja. Early on, they were identified with the seven stars of the Big Dipper, which had special significance in some Vedic rites.

The Chinese remember the seven sages of the "bamboo grove," a group of scholars and poets living in the middle of the second century A.D. They included Hsi K'ang, Hsiang Hsiu, Liu Ling, Kuo Hsiang, Shan T'ao, Wang Jung, and Yuan Chi.

Following suit, the Greeks honored Bias of Priene, Chilo of Sparta, Cleobulus of Lindos, Periander of Corinth, Pittacus of Mytilene, Solon of Athens, and Thales of Miletus as their seven wise men.

THE EIGHT IMMORTALS OF TAOISM

Taoism, one of China's four major spiritual traditions, denotes the ultimate Reality by the name *tao,* meaning "way." The supreme Way is eternal, unchanging Being and the origin of the finite, ever-changing universe. Through the dynamics of *yin* and *yang,* the female and male cosmic principles, the tao creates all phenomena. Whereas the tao is perfectly harmonious, the cosmos is in a state of constant disequilibrium.

The human body, as a product of the unstable universe, contains disharmonious forces that ultimately lead to death. Taoism teaches that these inbuilt forces can be checked and the seemingly inevitable progression toward extinction can be reversed: The human being is, in essence, the immortal tao.

In contrast to the Gnostics, the Taoists do not believe in a radical distinction between matter and spirit. Thus they also do not envisage liberation as the voluntary, conscious separation of the spirit from the body. Rather they maintain that the body, as an epitome of the cosmos, is a multilevel structure that can be harmonized and transformed by its own inherent energies. Through proper moral discipline, dieting, exercising, breath control, and special sexual techniques that conserve the seminal fluid, the Taoists seek to transmute the body. They are spiritual alchemists. For them immortality is accomplished by the combination of spirit and vitality. Their union is thought to produce the seed of immortality, leading to the full manifestation of the golden light within. The goal of Taoism is to create the indestructible diamond body. Upon this attainment, the physical body is neither existent nor nonexistent.

Popular belief recognizes a group of eight immortals (*pa-hsien*), which are often represented in art and literature. The earliest references to eight immortals stem from the T'ang dynasty (618–906 A.D.). However, the current octet was established during the Ming dynasty (1368–1644 A.D.). It includes the following figures, listed in the traditional order:

1. Li T'ieh-kuai ("Li with the Iron Crutch"), who had an abscess on his leg that was healed by the beautiful Hsi Wang-mu ("Royal Mother of the West"). She also initiated him into the secrets of Taoism. He is commonly depicted holding an iron crutch and a pumpkin filled with a magical draft.

2. Chang Kuo-lao (died between 742 and 746 A.D.), who had a magic donkey that could travel a thousand miles a day and then be reduced to a handkerchief. His characteristic symbol is a drum.

3. Ts'ao Kuo-chiu (died 1097 A.D.), who was a brother-in-law of an emperor of the Sung dynasty. His emblem is a pair of castanets.

4. Han Hsiang-tzu (T'ang dynasty), who was a nephew of the famous writer and statesman Han Yü. His symbol is a flute, a bouquet of flowers, or a peach.

5. Lü Tung-pin (born 798 A.D.), whose emblem is a sword—the magic sword given to him by a fire dragon—that destroys passion and ignorance.

6. Ho Hsien-ku (T'ang dynasty), who is the only female immortal of the group. She was a breatharian and able to fly through the air.

7. Lan Ts'ai-ho, who is depicted wearing the attire of a beggar, carrying a basket of flowers in one hand. Sometimes he is given female features.

8. Chung Li-ch'üan (Han dynasty, 206 B.C.–220 A.D.), who was an army officer before learning the secret arts of Taoism. The emblem of this portly, bald immortal with a beard down to his navel is a fan.

The Chinese also know of "eight immortals of the winecup," a group of Taoist poets who were known as much for their fine poetry as for their hard drinking. Among them is Li Po, one of China's great poetic geniuses who, according to one account, will write one hundred poems for a jugful of wine. The profligate ways of these poets drive home the point that repression of sensuous experience is not the Taoist approach, which, rather, consists in the cultivation of naturalness or spontaneity.

THE EIGHT DAYS OF THE
JEWISH FESTIVAL OF HANUKKAH

In the second century B.C., the Syrian king Antiochus IV persecuted the Jews and desecrated the altar in the Temple of Jerusalem. After Judah the Maccabee succeeded in re-capturing the temple in 165 B.C., the altar was rededicated. Hanukkah ("Dedication") is celebrated annually in memory of this event.

The festival lasts for eight days, following the stipulation in I Maccabee 4:59 that "the dedication of the altar should be observed with gladness and joy for eight days, beginning with the twenty-fifth day of the month of Chislev [December]." According to the Talmud, the reason that Hanukkah extends over an eight-day period is that when the Temple was rededicated the oil lamps miraculously stayed lit for eight whole days, even though the oil supply should have run out after the first day.

Hanukkah is inaugurated by kindling the lights of an eight-branched candlestick—one light on the first day, two on the second, and so on. The festivities include scriptural readings, singing hymns like the *Maoz Tzur* ("Rock of Ages"), reciting psalms, playing children's games, notably the four-sided spinning top (*dreidl*), performing Hanukkah plays, eating oil-dipped foods, and not least, gift giving.

THE EIGHT LIMBS OF CLASSICAL YOGA

Yoga is within Hinduism what Sufism is within Islam, the Kabbalah within Judaism, and Gnosticism within Christianity. No one knows exactly how old Yoga is, but its roots reach back into Vedic times, over four thousand years ago. For many centuries its teachings were orally transmitted. Then, probably in the second century A.D. (or, according to some scholars, in the third century B.C.), Patanjali compiled the *Yoga-Sutra* ("Aphorisms of Yoga"). This compilation, consisting of 195 aphorisms (or 196 in some editions), had the purpose of serving students as a memory aid to the philosophy and practice of Yoga.

Patanjali's extremely terse formulations acquired immense popularity, and his sophisticated treatment of Yoga was widely accepted as the classic statement of the yogic point of view—hence "Classical Yoga." It took its proud place among the six systems of Hindu metaphysics. Patanjali's teaching is often referred to as the eight-limbed Yoga (*ashta-anga-yoga*), because he provided the best definitions of the eight principal "limbs" (*anga*) of the yogic path.

The eight constituent practices, or "limbs," are:

1. Moral observance (*yama,* literally "restraint"), which consists of the five virtues of nonharming (*ahimsa*), truthfulness (*satya*), nonstealing (*asteya*), chastity (*brahmacarya*), and greedlessness (*aparigraha*). These constitute the yogi's "great vow" and are to be practiced on all levels of existence (or consciousness), irrespective of time, place, or circumstance.

2. Self-restraint (*niyama*), which comprises purity (*shauca*), contentment (*samtosha*), asceticism (*tapas*), study (*svadhyaya*), and devotion to the Lord (*ishvara-pranidhana*).

3. Posture (*asana*), by which Patanjali meant certain meditation postures that keep the body comfortably stable while the mind is intensely focused inward.

4. Breath control (*pranayama*), which entails more than the mere regulation of the body's oxygen intake. The term *prana* literally means "life" and denotes the cosmic life force that surrounds and interpenetrates everything. The yogis understood early on that mental activity is closely connected with the breath, and the breath is the

outermost aspect of the life force. By regulating (harmonizing and slowing down) the breath, and thus the life force manifesting in the body, the yogi simultaneously balances and decelerates the mind. In this way, attention becomes like a laser beam, opening up inner vision and, ultimately, leading to the recovery of the transcendental witness–Self (*purusha*).

5. Sensory inhibition (*pratyahara*), which involves the systematic withdrawal of the senses from the external world, leading to a state of increasing inwardness.

6. Concentration (*dharana*), which is the pin-pointing of attention to a select object.

7. Meditation (*dhyana*), which is a spontaneous deepening of concentration, whereby arising thoughts revolve naturally around the chosen object of concentration (be it an idea, a sound, or an image).

8. Ecstasy (*samadhi*), which is the sudden coalescence of consciousness with the contemplated object. In samadhi, the customary boundary between subject and object is broken down, and the yogi *becomes,* in consciousness, what he meditates on. There are degrees of this ecstatic merging, depending on what level of reality identification with the object is achieved and whether or not thoughts (or awarenesses) are present. The highest level of merging is the supraconscious ecstasy (*asamprajnata-samadhi*), which is free from thought forms and in which the unconscious tendency to focus on external reality is gradually overcome.

The yogi aims at quieting his inner world to the point where it is as clear as a calm, ripple-free pond. When this is accomplished, through hard discipline and divine grace, the true nature of the human being reveals itself: the transcendental Self, or spirit, beyond all qualities. The Self, our true identity, always merely witnesses the incessant activities of Nature (including the mind). It never gets involved in Nature's games, yet it appears to do so from the perspective of unenlightenment, for the unenlightened being operates with a false sense of identity ("I am male/female, of such-and-such age, color, background, etc.").

The purpose of the eight-limbed yogic path is, step by step, to liberate the practitioner from that mistaken identity. All the practices of the eight limbs can be viewed as means to that end. When the mind is silenced, the true Self can emerge. For Patanjali, the moment of full emergence, or liberation, coincides with the shedding of the physical body. Liberation is "aloneness" (*kaivalya*), pure witnessing, but this aloneness is not loneliness, for the many transcendental Selves are all omnipresent and eternal and hence flawlessly identical.

THE NOBLE EIGHTFOLD PATH OF THE BUDDHA

Long before Patanjali, in the sixth century B.C., the prince Gautama abandoned his privileged lifestyle and, at the age of twenty-nine, did what thousands of others were doing in those days: he became an ascetic, searching for convincing answers to the enigma of human existence. He tried every form of penance and nearly starved himself to death, but he remained unsatisfied with his spiritual attainments, though they were considerable. In the end, he gave up his fierce asceticism and, remembering a spontaneous childhood experience, sat himself beneath a poplar-fig tree intent on meditating until he had broken through. Four weeks later, he got up, fully enlightened. The miracle of inner transformation had occurred: He was a *buddha,* an "awakened" being.

Soon the thirty-five-year-old master could be heard preaching with great inner strength and authority on the four noble truths of Buddhism. The fourth truth was the noble eightfold path, which the Buddha offered as a way out of ignorance and suffering. The eight constituent practices of the Buddha's path are as follows (with Pali equivalents in parentheses):

1. Right view (*samma-ditthi*), which consists in a thorough understanding of the four noble truths and the recognition that the ordinary sense of self ("I, me, mine") is illusory.

2. Right resolve (*samma-sankappa*), which comprises three elements, namely the resolve to renounce the world, to be benevolent, and to observe nonharming toward all creatures.

3. Right speech (*samma-vaca*), which consists in the cultivation of speech that is true and the avoidance of gossip and verbal abuse.

4. Right conduct (*samma-kammanta*), which comprises the careful observance of three important prohibitions, namely not to take life, not to steal, and not to indulge.

5. Right livelihood (*samma-ajiva*), which implies adopting an occupation that does not involve harming others. Thus Buddhists cannot serve in the military or be hunters and fishermen.

6. Right effort (*samma-vayama*), which is explained as the cultivation of wholesome inner attitudes and the refraining from unwholesome attitudes.

7. Right awareness (*samma-sati*), which means the cultivation of mindfulness in regard to the processes of body and mind.

8. Right meditation (*samma-samadhi*), which comprises the practice of all kinds of concentration and meditation exercises, including the four stages of Buddhist meditation and the four levels of formless realization in Buddhism.

The first two practices are said to relate to wisdom, the next three to morality, and the last three to meditation. Gautama the Buddha proffered the noble eightfold path as a royal road to "extinction," or *nirvana* (Pali: *nibbana*)—not total nothingness but the extinction of desire, which lies at the bottom of suffering. However, the Pali scriptures also know of individuals who attained nirvana after a single instruction in the Buddhist teaching. In their case, insight alone sufficed to break the stranglehold of the false self-sense. Others, less qualified, must be prepared to tread the path lifetime after lifetime, but their liberation or awakening is also assured.

THE EIGHT CHRISTIAN BEATITUDES

In his famous Sermon on the Mount, Jesus of Nazareth talked about the benefits granted by God to those who turn to him with faith and live their lives in the divine light. These benefits, or blessings, are known as the *beatitudes* (from the Latin word *beatus* or "blessed"). In the gospels of Matthew and Luke, where this sermon is reported, the Greek word *makarios* is used. Appropriately, this term previously had been used to denote not ordinary happiness but the happiness of the gods. For the happiness promised by Jesus is not temporary joy, or pleasure, but everlasting bliss in the company of God. Those who follow in the footsteps of Jesus, practicing the *imitatio Christi,* will have a foretaste of the heavenly bliss to come.

According to St. Matthew's version, paraphrased here, the eight beatitudes are:

1. Blessed are the poor in spirit, for theirs is the kingdom of heaven.

2. Blessed are those who mourn, for they shall be comforted.

3. Blessed are the meek, for they shall inherit the earth.

4. Blessed are those who hunger and thirst after righteousness, for they shall be filled.

5. Blessed are the merciful, for they shall obtain mercy.

6. Blessed are those who are pure at heart, for they shall see God.

7. Blessed are the peacemakers, for they shall be called the children of God.

8. Blessed are those who are persecuted for their righteousness, for theirs is the kingdom of heaven.

This version differs from that of St. Luke in that it is more spiritualized, less focused on material life. Although St. Luke's list is not as elaborate, he provides a set of woes matching the beatitudes. Thus he has Jesus say, "Woe unto you who are rich!" etc. Both versions are practical admonitions to place earthly life in proper perspective and not to look for shortlived pleasure and profit when the real reward waits in heaven.

THE EIGHT AUSPICIOUS SYMBOLS OF UNIVERSAL RULERSHIP IN BUDDHISM

The Buddhists regard the Buddha as a universal monarch, similar to the Christian idea of Jesus as "King of the World." They associate the following eight symbols with this idea of spiritual dominion:

1. the parasol, which is a symbol of royal dignity;
2. the two golden fish, which are joined at the head and the tail, symbolizing endless good fortune;
3. the conch shell, which is a symbol of victory;
4. the lotus flower, suggesting purity but also self-creation and autonomy;
5. the furled banner, which is an emblem of spiritual victory and protection;
6. the vase, which is filled with the nectar of immortality;
7. the knot of eternity, a lattice-like geometric design that is similar in its significance to the mathematical symbol numeral 8 placed horizontally;
8. the eight-spoked wheel of the Buddha's teaching, which is a symbol of completeness or wholeness, since the eightfold path liberates one from bondage and suffering.

In China, these eight emblems, known as *ashta-mangalas,* are often placed on lotus-shaped pedestals in front of Buddha statues.

SEE ALSO The Thirty-Two Marks of a Buddha

THE EIGHT GREAT PSYCHIC POWERS OF YOGA

The Yoga scriptures again and again refer to the eight great paranormal or magical powers, the *ashta-siddhis,* as abilities possessed by the greatest masters. These eight powers are:

1. *Animan,* the power to make oneself infinitely small at will;
2. *Mahiman,* the ability to grow infinitely large in an instant;
3. *Laghiman,* or levitation, defeating the law of gravity;
4. *Prapti* (literally "extension"), the ability to contact any object regardless of its distance, such as touching the moon with a fingertip;
5. *Prakamya,* or irresistible will, such as diving into solid ground and moving about as if it were water;
6. *Vashitva* (literally "mastery"), or total control over the elements;
7. *Ishitritva,* or lordship over the entire universe, including the creation and destruction of the material elements;
8. *Kamavasayitva,* or the instant fulfillment of all one's wishes.

The Sanskrit term *siddhi* can mean "attainment," "accomplishment," or "perfection." In the metaphysical literature of the Hindus, this term is often applied to the ultimate spiritual realization of liberation, or enlightenment. However, it is also used to denote the major paranormal abilities that accrue to the adept by virtue of his or her Self-realization. In other words, the magical attainments are viewed as byproducts of spiritual perfection. They come to the adept unbidden. Sometimes they are even regarded as integral to, and a sure sign of, Self-realization.

These *maha-siddhis* or "great powers" must be distinguished from lesser paranormal abilities, such as remote viewing (*dura-darshana*) or clairaudience (*divya-shrotra*), which can be consciously cultivated by anyone, even those who have no spiritual orientation at all.

Strictly speaking, the eight great powers are powers of the Self, not of the ego-personality. Hence they cannot possibly be abused for selfish ends as can the lesser paranormal abilities. However, this did not prevent popular imagination from inventing many entertaining tales about yogis who, in a fit of anger, stopped the sun in its course, plunging the earth into total darkness, or even started to dissolve the universe by an act of sheer will. Some metaphysical texts show a more sophisticated understanding, making it clear that the eight powers pertain not to the physical world but to a more subtle dimension of existence.

It is sometimes held that Patanjali, the compiler of the *Yoga-Sutra,* warned against the siddhis as a possible obstacle to higher states of consciousness. This view is incorrect. His admonition only concerns a certain type of paranormal activity, such as clairvoyance, which involves focusing one's attention on the external reality rather than allowing it to turn within.

THE EIGHT TRIGRAMS OF THE I CHING

The *I Ching* ("Book of Changes") consists of eight fundamental trigrams, invented by Fu Hsi five thousand years
ago, together with the main text authored two thousand
years later by King Wen and his son, the Duke of Chou.

Fu Hsi (2953–2838 B.C.) was the first of five emperors belonging to the legendary era. His mother conceived him in a miraculous way and gave birth to him after
a pregnancy lasting twelve years. He was a culture hero of
the first order, teaching his subjects how to hunt, fish,
herd, and make silk and musical instruments. Inspired by
the markings on the back of a tortoise, he created the eight
trigrams on which the whole divinatory system of the *I
Ching* depends. Each trigram consists of three broken and/
or unbroken horizontal lines.

Fu Hsi arranged the eight trigrams (*pa-kua*) into two
groups, one representing the feminine principle (*yin*), the
other representing the masculine principle (*yang*). To the
former group belong the symbols *sun* (wind), *k'an* (water),
ken (mountain), and *k'un* (earth); the latter includes the
signs *chen* (thunder), *li* (fire), *tui* (gaiety), and *ch'ien* (heaven).
(The spelling of Chinese names varies widely.) The most
important trigrams are the symbols for heaven and earth, as
their mixing is thought to yield the remaining six trigrams.

Probably the ingenuity of King Wen and the Duke of
Chou is responsible for the creation of the 64 hexagrams,
which is the total number of symbols resulting from combining the eight trigrams. Each hexagram is a unit of two
trigrams, one placed above the other. The *I Ching* has been
labelled an oracular computer, which faithfully reflects the
nature of the present moment in the never-ending flux of
events and offers practical wisdom geared to that

moment. The hexagrams capture the essence of human experience, though the traditional interpretations of each hexagram are overdetermined by Chinese culture, notably courtly life. Modern users of the *I Ching* have begun to reinterpret the hexagrams in terms of current psychological and cultural patterns.

The appropriate hexagram for a given moment is determined by casting off forty-nine yarrow sticks (taking about thirty minutes) or throwing three coins (taking less than a minute). The idea behind this ritual practice is that the hand unconsciously moves in accord with the psycho-cosmic forces of the present moment. The attitude of the questioner must be meditative or centered, and he or she must have a real question to which an answer is sought.

C. G. Jung, in his foreword to Richard Wilhelm's acclaimed translation of the *I Ching,* called his work a "great and singular book." He also observed that the *Book of Changes* "insists upon self-knowledge throughout," that is, it is not for the immature or lazy individual who hopes for a quick fix. The purpose of the *I Ching* is to harmonize the questioner's being with heaven. More than an oracle, this ancient work is a reflective mirror in which the thoughtful person may discover inner truths.

~9~

THE NINE ORDERS OF ANGELS IN CHRISTIANITY

The belief in luminous spirit beings who dwell in higher realms that are invisible to the ordinary person is universal. In Christianity, these beings of light are called "angels." The word stems from the Greek *angelos,* meaning "messenger." The ancient Greeks, however, applied the term *angelos* to their divinities, notably those of the underworld that was the home of the dead. The supreme deity, Zeus, was called *agathos angelos,* "the good angel." The Hebrew term in the Old Testament is *mal'ak* and, like *angelos,* designated both human and nonhuman messengers.

According to Judeo-Christian and also Islamic doctrine, angels are higher beings who serve God and occasionally act as his messengers to humanity. Angels inform, guide, protect, or warn humans. Sometimes they appear only as voices, at other times they make themselves visible, occasionally even assuming human form. Thus angels prevented Abraham from sacrificing his son Isaac; guided the Hebrews to the promised land after their exodus from Egypt under Moses; revealed secrets about the

161

future to the prophets Zechariah, Ezekiel, and Daniel; fed Elijah in the wilderness; helped Jesus during his forty days in the wilderness and again at the time of his agony in the Garden; revealed the mystery of Jesus' resurrection to Mary Magdalene at the tomb; revealed God's will to the prophet Muhammad and prevented him from committing suicide when he feared ostracism for being a religious ecstatic (*kahin*); announced to Joan of Arc that she was destined to save her country.

In their divine commission to promote the good in the world, angels are sometimes assigned the task of destruction, as when an angel caused a pestilence among the Israelites or another angel killed 185,000 Assyrians for attacking the holy city of Jerusalem.

Angels are creatures of God but are immortal and hence do not need to reproduce. The early Christian Church Fathers believed that angels possessed an ethereal body. However, around 500 A.D., Dionysius introduced the idea that angels are immaterial entities. Nothing is known about Dionysius ("the Aeropagate"), who was deeply affected by Neoplatonism, but his writings greatly influenced medieval Christian thought. He believed that the divine Light is passed through a hierarchy of angelic beings before reaching humanity in stepped-down form suitable for the material world.

The angelology of Dionysius distinguishes nine types of angels organized into three hierarchic levels. The first level comprises the Seraphim, the Cherubim, and the Thrones. The Seraphim are the highest order of angelic beings. According to Dionysius, the Seraphim ("those who burn") eternally circumambulate God, communicating his light to the lower rungs in the great chain of being. The Hebrew prophet Isaiah described them as having a human form with six wings. These can be identified with the seven lights mentioned in Revelation, which burn brightly before God's throne.

Next in line are the Cherubim ("those who are full of wisdom"). Two gold-covered wooden Cherubim guarded the inner sanctuary of the first Temple of Jerusalem, their huge wings touching above the ark. In the vision of the prophet Ezekiel, God's throne is held up by the wings of four Cherubim. The four have human form but the faces of a man, a lion, an ox, and an eagle respectively. In St. John's vision, they had eyes everywhere, this being a sign of their omniscience.

The Thrones are the next order below the Cherubim. They are the twenty-four crowned elders, who are seated on seats before God's throne, as described in St. John's Revelation. They are ever ready to bow their heads and renounce their crowns before God.

The second level consists of Dominations, Virtues, and Powers. The names of these angelic beings suggest their specific functions in the celestial hierarchy.

The third level includes Principalities, Archangels, and Angels. The precise functions of these different levels and orders are only known to God, and they are said to be a mystery for mortals.

This consideration would be incomplete without mentioning Lucifer ("Bearer of Light"), the fallen angel. Once the most perfect angelic servant of God, Lucifer was banished from heaven for challenging God's authority. The name "Satan" captures this opposition, for it means "adversary."

~ 10 ~

THE TEN BIBLICAL NAMES OF GOD

Naming the nameless mystery, the great Reality beyond all forms, has been one of the paradoxical passions of the human mind. Mystics of all ages have affirmed that the Ultimate cannot be captured in words, and yet they have sung its praises in a thousand songs.

The Old Testament mentions a number of sacred names of God, each suggesting a different aspect of his nature and a particular relationship to humankind. The most important of them was Yahweh, written in Hebrew YHWH, known as the tetragrammaton. This is God's name for himself, which he first used when addressing Moses at the burning bush on Mount Sinai. He even proffered an explanation for it, saying it meant "I am what I am": God as a perfectly self-sufficient and self-determining being.

The names of God were later systematized in the Kabbalah, which knows of ten principal names, associated with the ten *sefiroth* of the Kabbalistic tree. The ten names in descending order are:

1. *Ehyeh Asher Ehyeh,* which is connected with *keter,* is the biblical "I Am What I Am";

2. *Yah* is the divine name associated with *chakhmah*;

3. *Yahweh,* which is associated with *binah,* is never pronounced in this way. The substitute name is Elohim, which is the masculine plural of a feminine noun, which suggests the androgynous nature of the Divine: God has both male and female attributes;

4. *El* is the divine name associated with *chesed*;

5. *Elohim* is connected with *gevurah*;

6. *Yahweh,* which is associated with *tiferet,* is here pronounced as Adonay;

7. *Adonay Tzevaot* is connected with *netzach*;

8. *Elohim Tzevaot* is connected with *hod*;

9. *Shaddai El Chai,* the Almighty Living God, is connected with *yesod*;

10. *Adonay* is connected with *malkhut,* the lowest of the ten sefiroth.

All names are regarded as elaborations of the original divine name—Yahweh. Each of the ten names is a signpost that refers back to one of the sefiroth, which are vessels for God's essence. For the Kabbalist the entire Torah (the first five books of the Old Testament) is not so much a narrative as a book of symbols that, when decoded, reveal God's handiwork in and through the ten sefiroth.

SEE ALSO The Ten Sefiroth of the Kabbalah

THE TEN FORMS OF THE GODDESS IN TANTRISM

Hindu Tantrism favors the Divine in its feminine aspect as the Goddess. According to some schools, the Goddess has ten great forms. They are all regarded as embodiments of wisdom, or higher knowledge, since worshipful contemplation of the Goddess leads to revelatory knowledge. This teaching is analogous to the Gnostic tradition of *sophia,* or "wisdom," as the feminine Divine. The Goddess is the source of spiritual insight and illumination, but, more than that, she *is* that wisdom. For higher knowledge guides the aspirant to the state of ecstatic merging with the Goddess, whereupon knower, knowledge, and known all coincide.

The ten forms of the Goddess, which are known as the *mahavidyas* or "great wisdoms," are as follows:

1. Kali—who is the primary form of the Goddess. She is dark, unpredictable, and threatening. Her skin is dark blue, and she wears a garland of skulls. She is traditionally associated with death and destruction. As her name suggests, she is the inexorable force behind time (*kala*) and change. But Kali is not merely destructive. She also is the movement of life. Properly understood, she is the great motivator behind growth, especially spiritual growth. For when we become aware of our mortality, we being to turn our attention to the Eternal. Time is a mighty teacher, and Kali is the mistress of time.

2. Tara—who is the saving aspect of the Goddess. She takes the devotee across the ocean of conditioned existence to the "other shore." Yet, like Kali, Tara is often depicted in a terrifying way—dancing on a corpse holding a severed head in one of her four hands. This is to remind worshippers that divine grace has its own agenda and that spiritual maturation means growing beyond the ego, which is neither easy nor pain-free. Tara is also invoked in difficult situations and is particularly associated with the sacred sound *om,* the primal vibration behind all creation.

3. Tripura Sundari—who stands for the essential beauty of the Goddess. Her beauty, however, transcends the beauty of all manifest forms or, rather, she *is* the beauty we admire when we delight in a beautiful flower, sunset, or work of art. She is called *tripura* or "triple city" because she rules the three states of consciousness—waking, dream, and deep sleep—but she herself is forever beyond them.

4. Bhuvaneshvari—who is the ruler of the universe, which is also the meaning of her name. She is infinite space, just as Kali is infinite time. If Kali is the power of action (*kriya-shakti*) and Tripura Sundari is the power of knowledge (*jnana-shakti*), Bhuvaneshvari is the power of the will (*iccha-shakti*). It is through divine will, or desire, that the universe exists. Thus she stands for the principle of creativity.

5. Bhairavi—who is a fierce, awesome form of the Goddess. She is depicted with bare breasts smeared with blood. She represents divine anger, the kind of fiery energy that demands change and self-transformation from the devotee. Her anger is always constructive. This is captured in iconography by her hand gestures: Two hands are in the gesture (*mudra*) of bestowing knowledge upon her worshippers, and two hands are in the gesture of granting protection or dispelling fear.

6. Chinnamasta—who is the Goddess with the severed (*chinna*) head (*masta*). She is portrayed headless, with blood spurting from her neck. This gruesome image is a powerful message to the devotee to cut off his or her own head, that is, to dissolve the conceptual mind so as to realize the transconceptual blissful Reality.

7. Dhumavati—who is the crone aspect of the Goddess. She is depicted as an old destitute hag: the archetypal

image of what mortals fear the most, which is the loss of life and the inevitable approach of old age and death. She is the divine smokescreen, revealing deeper levels of existence by obscuring others. Hence her name "Smoky." The trouble and misfortune she brings always contain the possibility of change for the better, of genuine growth and happiness.

8. Bagalamukhi—who is ravishingly beautiful. She spellbinds her devotees with her lovely form. She is portrayed with a golden complexion and carrying a club in one hand. The club suggests that this aspect of the Goddess is not without its sting. With her cudgel she demolishes all foes: all the false ideas harbored in the devotee's mind. Her great power is that of stoppage (*stambhana*): of mind, speech, and negative energies. She is rightly called the "brahmic weapon."

9. Matangi—who is often depicted as a beautiful woman with a dark green complexion, seated on a gem-studded throne and holding various weapons and a lute in her four hands. She is the patron of the arts. She also is described as being an outcast, because audible speech, for which she stands, is inherently "polluted" or limited. Yet, Matangi empowers the devotee to look beyond mere appearances and discover the uncaused primordial sound.

10. Kamalatmika—who is of the nature of the lotus flower (*kamala*). The lotus symbolizes purity. Although this flower grows out of mud, its beautiful blossom floats above the water. Kamalatmika is depicted as a lovely golden-hued woman seated on an open lotus, making the gestures of granting boons and freedom from fear with her four hands. She represents the Goddess in the fullness of her graceful aspect.

The ten Goddesses embody both the frightful and the beautiful aspects of the Divine. However, they are not meant to be exhaustive representations of the feminine principle of Reality, and Hinduism knows of many more manifestations of the Goddess. But these ten have been singled out for intense meditation and visualization practice in Tantrism.

THE TEN DIVINE INCARNATIONS IN HINDUISM

The names of God in the various spiritual traditions can be regarded as manifestations of the Divine by which the gulf between Creator and creature is bridged. Some traditions hold that the Divine actually sends forth from out of its sublime immensity a pure spirit clothed in some creaturely form. For instance, Christianity worships Jesus of Nazareth, the Christ, as such a manifestation of the Divine. But long before Christians began to flock around Jesus as the "anointed" (*christos*) Messiah, the Hindus pondered the profound mystery of the multiple manifestations or "incarnations" of Vishnu, the supreme Godhead. They are called *avataras* in Sanskrit, which means "descents."

An avatara is a divine emanation issuing directly from the ultimate Being. He (there have been no female descents) is not born as the result of karma accumulated in previous lives, but by virtue of a divine fiat. The avatara is conscious of his spiritual origin and comes with a specific mission, namely to reestablish the divine order in the world whenever humanity has strayed from the path.

The followers of Vishnu—the Vaishnavas—know of ten such embodiments of the Divine, which intervened in the world process in successive eras. They are:

1. Matsya ("Fish")—who saved Manu Satyavrata, the seventh law giver and founder of present-day humanity, from the great flood. Manu found a small fish in the water brought to him for ablutions. The fish asked him for protection, which Manu granted. The fish rapidly grew bigger and had to be placed in larger and larger containers, and Manu tenderly looked after its needs. Finally, when only the ocean itself could hold it, Manu recognized it as an incarnation of God Vishnu himself. Matsya blessed Manu, warning him of the impending deluge and directed him to construct a ship. When the flood arrived, Matsya pulled the ship, which had all the sages, plants, and animals on board, to safety.

2. Kurma ("Tortoise")—who was instrumental in recovering the nectar of immortality and other articles of power that had been lost during the deluge. He also made sure that these articles did not fall into the hands of the demonic beings of the cosmos who were engaged in a fierce tug-of-war with the gods.

3. Varaha ("Boar")—who lifted the earth from the world ocean into which it had been hurled by the demon Hiranyaksha ("Golden Eye").

4. Narasimha ("Man Lion")—who saved Prahlada, an ardent devotee, from persecution by his evil father, King Hiranyakashipu. The demonic king had been granted a boon by God Brahma, which made it impossible for him to be killed by day or by night, by god, human being, or beast, inside or outside his palace. Vishnu incarnated in a form that was neither completely human nor completely animal. He manifested inside of a pillar at twilight, and then destroyed Hiranyakashipu with his powerful claws.

5. Vamana ("Dwarf")—reclaimed, in three giant strides, the world from the demon Bali, who had acquired dominion over it through his incredible penance. In one step, Vamana covered the whole earth; with his second step he reclaimed the heavens, and with his third step he pushed Bali into the nether region where he rightfully belonged.

6. Parashu Rama ("Rama with the Ax")—who recovered the spiritual leadership of the brahmins which had been usurped by the warrior estate.

7. Rama ("Charming") or Ramacandra ("Charming Moon")—who rescued his chaste wife, Sita, from the clutches of the demon Ravana. This story is told in enormous detail in the *Ramayana*, one of India's two great national epics.

8. Krishna ("Puller")—who was born at the beginning of the Dark Age or *kali-yuga* and destroyed many demons, including the evil King Kamsa. Krishna was the teacher of Prince Arjuna, and their spiritual dialogue on the battlefield is recorded in the *Bhagavad-Gita*, which is a portion of India's second great national epic, the *Mahabharata*.

9. Buddha ("Awakened")—who preserved the purity of the Vedic tradition by proclaiming all kinds of false paths to attract the unworthy. Some Hindu authorities deny that this Buddha refers to Gautama, the founder of Buddhism, but they are probably wrong.

10. Kalki ("Pastor")—who, prophecy has it, will appear riding a white horse and holding a blazing sword. Kalki, or Kalkin, is thought of as the avatara who will establish the next Golden Age.

What is remarkable about this list is that it includes three nonhuman incarnations and one half-human incarnation. Only the last six are fully human.

Some Hindu authorities recognize sixteen, twenty-two, or even twenty-three incarnations. Others claim that the incarnations of the Divine are countless, and today not a few Hindus look upon Jesus as an avatara. The number of incarnations is of little importance and what matters is the metaphysical principle behind them: The Divine is not utterly separated from the world but is actively interested in its welfare.

THE TEN COMMANDMENTS IN THE JUDEO-CHRISTIAN TRADITION

About 3,300 years ago, Moses led the Israelites out of their Egyptian captivity. For forty years, he and his people wandered in the wilderness of Sinai in search of the promised land, which he never lived to see. While in Midian, he climbed Mount Sinai (presumably Jebel Musa) where he encountered Yahweh, the Lord, manifesting as a fire that wrapped the Mount in smoke.

A voice addressed him, uttering the famous biblical statement "I am the Lord thy God." Then Moses, the prophet, received detailed religious and moral instructions on behalf of his people. These included the famous ten commandments, which form the backbone of the Judaic and Christian moral tradition.

Subsequently God asked Moses a second time to climb to the top of Mount Sinai. This time he stayed for forty days, and on the seventh day, Yahweh revealed himself in a blazing bush, shining so brightly that Moses had to avert his eyes.

On this occasion, he gave Moses two stone tablets on which were engraved on both sides the ten commandments. He also gave him specific instructions about how the tablets were to be stored. On his return, Moses found his people worshipping a golden calf, completely forgetful of the Lord's covenant. In anger, he smashed the two tablets. He asked those who were faithful to Yahweh to stand beside him and for all others to be slaughtered. Three thousand people met their death that day.

Yahweh asked Moses to cut two stone tablets similar to the first two and to ascend Mount Sinai one more time so that God could inscribe the ten commandments on them. The commandments, which are usually known in the form given in Exodus (20:3–17), are as follows (Authorized King James Version):

1. Thou shalt have no other gods before me.

2. Thou shalt not make unto thee any graven image, or any likeness of any thing that is in heaven above or that is in the earth beneath, or that is in the water under the earth. Thou shalt not bow down thyself to them, nor serve them.

3. Thou shalt not take the name of the Lord thy God in vain.

4. Remember the sabbath day, to keep it holy.

5. Honor thy father and thy mother.

6. Thou shalt not kill.

7. Thou shalt not commit adultery.

8. Thou shalt not steal.

9. Thou shalt not bear false witness against thy neighbor.

10. Thou shalt not covet thy neighbor's house; thou shalt not covet thy neighbor's wife.

The ten commandments are numbered differently in the Roman Catholic and the Lutheran Churches on the one hand and the Talmud, the Eastern Orthodox, and the Reformed Churches on the other hand. The former combine the second and the third commandment but treat the injunction against coveting the neighbor's wife and against coveting his house as two separate commandments.

THE TEN SEFIROTH IN THE KABBALAH

The Jewish mystical tradition, which was originally referred to as the "hidden wisdom" (*chakhmah nistrarah*) and later came to be known as the Kabbalah ("Tradition"), is based on an emanationist metaphysics. That is to say, it maintains that the universe emerged out of the Divine while still remaining a part of it. This emanation, or outpouring, is thought to occur as a consequence of the combined agency of ten principles, called the *sefiroth,* which have sometimes been venerated as high spiritual beings in their own right. They are at once qualities and powers of the Divine and are referred to as the "face of God."

Each *sefirah* ("counting" or "telling") has a specific function, yet is part of an interpenetrating whole formed by all ten sefiroth. Together they not only create the objective universe in its multiple dimensions but also form the primordial human being, the Adam Kadmon. In the order of their emergence out of the Divine, the ten sefiroth are:

1. *Keter* ("Crown"), which is pure, indivisible being, the Creator's will that precedes all creation;

2. *Chakhmah* ("Wisdom"), which is the primordial masculine principle of activity. Often called the "Father" of the other sefiroth, it is the blueprint for all subsequent creation;

3. *Binah* ("Understanding"), which is the primordial feminine principle of receptivity. It is the level of existence of the twenty-four Elders, who have absolute knowledge of all destinies;

4. *Chesed* ("Mercy"), which radiates the Divine in all directions, limited only by *gevurah*;

5. *Gevurah* ("Justice"), which represents God's ability to limit his infinite mercy. Without this self-limiting function, the existence of the universe would not be possible;

6. *Tiferet* ("Beauty"), which represents the state of harmony among the sefiroth. This also corresponds to the state of the witnessing awareness beyond the ordinary mind;

7. *Netzach* ("Victory"), which is said to be one of the means by which God governs the world, the other being *hod*. It is the reality of all forms, sounds, scents, and colors, and the base for artistic inspiration;

8. *Hod* ("Glory"), which is the realm of knowledge and of the archangels;

9. *Yesod* ("Foundation"), which is the abode of angels (the *kerubim*);

10. *Malkhut* ("Kingdom"), which is the final vessel of the Divine and the means by which the other sefiroth realize their potential. It stands for the flawless harmony between the ten sefiroth.

These ten principles, also spoken of as the ten lights, are arranged into a distinct pattern that is knows as the Kabbalistic tree of life. This structure is composed of three triads and a tenth principle combining the qualities of all. Keter, as the name suggests, is at the crown of the tree and forms the first triad together with chakmah and binah. Beneath them is the second triad constituted by chesed, gevurah, and tiferet. The third triad is made up of netzach, hod, and yesod. Finally, at the base of the tree, is malkhut. It is also called *shekhinah,* the spirit of God present in the world.

Beyond the tree of life is *ain sof* ("No Thing"), the Divine. Thus the Kabbalah teaches both the transcendence and the immanence of God. This teaching is crucial to Kabbalistic practice, which aims at discovering the divine spirit within.

THE TEN STAGES OF THE LIFE OF A BODHISATTVA IN BUDDHISM

In Buddhism, a *buddha* is an awakened being who has reached "extinction" (*nirvana*) by his own power. An *arahant,* or "worthy one," is someone who has attained the same supreme condition through the instruction of a buddha. In Hinayana (or Theravada) Buddhism, which is prevalent in Sri Lanka, the arahant is held up as the noblest ideal to which human beings can aspire.

Mahayana Buddhism, which originated in the centuries immediately preceding the Christian era, is based on a different ideal—that of the *bodhisattva.* This Sanskrit term means literally "awakened being." A bodhisattva is a person (or nonhuman being) who is utterly committed to the ideal of spiritual illumination (*bodhi*), or buddhahood.

However, a bodhisattva vows to defer his or her own ultimate liberation until all beings are liberated. He or she is motivated solely by compassion (*karuna*) for those countless human and nonhuman entities throughout the universe who are suffering because they do not know that, in essence, they are free and awakened. The self-chosen task of the bodhisattva is to relieve the pain of others, and by transferring his or her own karmic merits, to bring them happiness, joy, and ultimate liberation. The bodhisattva's unselfish service yields continuous karmic merit, which is replenished with every act of compassion, and thus is inexhaustible.

The Mahayana scriptures describe ten states (*bhumi*) of the bodhisattva's path. The descriptions vary from text to text but, in principle, the stages are as follows:

1. The joyous stage (*pramudita-bhumi*): Once the impulse toward enlightenment, called *bodhicitta,* has awakened in a person, he or she takes the vow of a bodhisattva. Filled with joy, the new bodhisattva dedicates himself or herself particularly to practicing the virtue of giving (*dana*).

2. The immaculate stage (*vimala-bhumi*): Here the bodhisattva perfects the virtue of self-discipline (*shila*).

3. The radiant stage (*prabhakari-bhumi*): As wisdom develops, giving the bodhisattva insight into the transitory and unsatisfactory nature of the world, he or she focuses on cultivating patience (*kshanti*).

4. The blazing stage (*arcishmati-bhumi*): This stage receives its name from the bodhisattva's practice of burning all the remnants of false ideas about the world. At this level, he or she cultivates exertion (*virya*), or will-power.

5. The extremely-difficult-to-conquer stage (*sudur-jaya-bhumi*): Here the bodhisattva struggles to achieve complete mastery in meditation (*dhyana*).

6. The facing stage (*abhimukhi-bhumi*): On this level, the bodhisattva's task is to perfect wisdom (*prajna*), which reveals to him or her the completely illusory nature of the self. Upon death, he or she is entitled to enter the condition of nirvana, but because of the bodhisattva vow he or she is fully prepared to make the ultimate sacrifice of postponing entrance into nirvana indefinitely. This stage is so called because the bodhisattva "faces" the sword of wisdom.

7. The far-going stage (*durangama-bhumi*): At this point, the incarnate bodhisattva becomes a transcendental bodhisattva who is freed from the limitations of a physical body and is capable of assuming any form at will. He cultivates the perfection of right method (*upaya*).

8. The immovable stage (*acala-bhumi*): Here the transcendental bodhisattva acquires the ability to transfer his or her karmic merit to unliberated beings. The bodhisattva becomes a graceful savior, perfecting his or her vow (*pranidhana*).

9. The good-thoughts stage (*sadhumati-bhumi*): The godlike bodhisattva continues to favor all unliberated beings with perfect vigor (*virya*). A bodhisattva of this order is Avalokiteshvara, who is worshipped throughout the Mahayana Buddhist world.

10. The cloud-of-substance stage (*dharmamegha-bhumi*): The bodhisattva attains to the perfection of knowledge (*jnana*). His or her transcendental body irradi-

ates the entire universe. Maitreya, the future buddha, is a bodhisattva of this crowning level.

Beyond these ten stages lies buddhahood. As the bodhisattva traverses through these levels of spiritual accomplishment and realization, he or she cultivates the ten virtues to perfection.

SEE ALSO The Six Virtue Perfections in Mahayana Buddhism

THE TEN OX–HERDING PICTURES OF ZEN

The ten ox-herding pictures (*jugyu-no-zu*) are a graphic representation of the various levels of understanding and illumination that the Zen practitioner traverses. Accompanied by a short text, they became very popular in Japan in the fourteenth and fifteenth centuries. There are many versions of these pictures, and the earliest versions consist of only five, six, or eight pictures.

The pictures, which show a herder and his ox or buffalo, are typically drawn each within a circle. In the Zen master Kaku-an Zhi-en (Chinese: Kuo-an Shih-yuan) version, the pictures depict the following ten stages:

1. searching for the ox (which has never really gone astray);
2. discovering the tracks (through study of the scriptures);
3. catching a first glimpse of the ox (grasping the essential teaching of the continuous presence of "it");
4. catching the ox (which, owing to the pressure of the outside world, is not easily tamed);

5. herding the ox (through control of the mind);

6. riding the ox home (after gaining equanimity);

7. forgetting the ox (which is no longer needed);

8. forgetting both ox and self (which are both equally dispensable);

9. returning to the origin (by simply abiding in perfect serenity, no longer identifying with the illusion-like change of the world);

10. entering the world with compassion.

At the last stage, the sage participates again in life, but from the vantage point of his realization. Unrecognized by others, but with a broad smile, he imperceptibly transforms other beings by his mere presence. As master Kaku-an puts it (in D. T. Suzuki's rendering):

> Bare-chested and bare-footed, he comes out into the
>   market place;
> Daubed with mud and ashes, how broadly he smiles!
> There is no need for the miraculous power of the gods,
> For he touches, and lo! the dead trees are in full bloom.

THE TEN BODILY GATES IN HINDUISM

All spiritual traditions agree that the human body is constructed in such a fashion that consciousness is constantly enticed to pay attention to the happenings of the external environment. The mechanism by which it is drawn into the outer reality is sensory perception. In Hinduism, the body is likened to a castle that has ten gates (*dvara*)—a metaphor that dates back to the *Atharva-Veda* of some four thousand years ago, which speaks of nine gates.

The gates are the bodily apertures through which the most direct and intense contact with the external world is made possible. The ten gates are the two eyes, two ears, two nostrils, the mouth, the opening of the urethra, the anus, and the sagittal suture at the crown of the head. Sometimes the navel is added as an eleventh gate.

From a spiritual point of view, the most important gate is the sagittal suture, which is formed by the junction of the two parietal bones of the skull. In young children the two bones are still separated, forming a soft area in the middle of the crown. This spot is also known as the "brahmic opening" (*brahma-randhra*) or the "wheel of extinction" (*nirvana-cakra*). Both technical names indicate that it is here that the individuated consciousness (*citta*) links up with the universal consciousness (*cit*). This is also the place through which the accomplished yogi may exit the body at will, either at the moment of death or in order to travel in consciousness outside the body.

In the esoteric model of the seven psychospiritual centers (*cakras*) in Tantrism, the gate at the crown of the head is designated as the thousand-petaled lotus (*sahasrara-cakra*). Activation of that center, through intense meditation or visualization and the deliberate manipulation of the life force (*prana*), can cause the sagittal suture to reopen.

SEE ALSO The Five Senses in Various Traditions

THE TWELVE LINKS OF DEPENDENT ORIGINATION
IN THERAVADA BUDDHISM

All the great spiritual traditions spawned on the Indian subcontinent share the belief that we have more than one life and that actions and even intentions in the present life have consequences for future embodiment. This is the notion of karma.

In Buddhism the doctrine of karma and reincarnation is complicated by the fact that the Buddha denied the existence of a permanent Self, such as the Hindu *atman.* This denial poses the question of what it is that survives death and becomes reembodiment. Insistent on rejecting the brahmanical idealism of the *Upanishads,* the Buddha proffered an ingenious solution to this seemingly intractable problem: the doctrine of dependent origination (*pratitya-samutpada*).

According to this doctrine, the continuity between one embodiment and the next is merely relative. There is no transmigrating subject, or soul (atman). Rather, certain conditions produce other conditions, which produce other conditions, and so on. This sequence is similar to the action of an atomic particle that smacks into another atomic particle, imparting some of its momentum and setting up a whole chain reaction. Life is constant motion, a continuous transference of energy. Yet, as the Buddhists see it, there is no one to ride on that wave of energy. The Pali canon has several versions of the doctrine of dependent origination. The best known consists of the following twelve linking factors (*nidana*):

1. Ignorance (*avidya*) gives rise to intentions;
2. Intentions (*samskara*) give rise to consciousness;
3. Consciousness (*vijnana*) gives rise to name and body;
4. Name and form (*nama-rupa*) give rise to the sixfold sphere of sense contact;
5. The sixfold sphere of sense contact (*shad-ayatana*) gives rise to actual contact;
6. Sensory contact (*sparsha*) gives rise to sensation;
7. Sensation (*vedana*) gives rise to craving;
8. Craving (*trishna*) gives rise to grasping;
9. Grasping (*upadana*) gives rise to becoming;
10. Becoming (*bhava*) gives rise to birth;
11. Birth (*jati*) gives rise to
12. Old age and death (*jara-marana*).

It is obvious from the series of twelve conditions that consciousness is merely one of the factors, not, as in some other schools, the primary cause of karma and reincarnation. There is no superconscious subject that witnesses the karmic process, inhabiting body after body. The conditional nexus only means to explain the fate of the empirical psyche, which is different in every incarnation. For the

Buddhist, the thought of an immortal self is precisely a product of ignorance, which is the source of the whole karmic nexus.

Nirvana is defined as the extinction of craving, the termination of all ignorance, which is the end of the entire cycle of rebirths, and thus of all suffering. The Buddha refused to say more about it, lest he should be misunderstood. It is intriguing that the Pali canon reports the Buddha as speaking about "his" numerous previous lives. This shows that, though there is no transmigrating soul, the chain of karmic events can be traced backward. At any rate, judging from the testimony of the Buddha's own life, as we know it from the early Buddhist scriptures, nirvana is clearly a desirable realization. Far from turning Gautama into a shadow of his former self, it made him whole and radiant—the "awakened one."

THE TWELVE REFLECTIONS IN JAINISM

In the Jaina tradition, the mendicant is expected to practice repeatedly the twelve reflections, which seek to pierce through the veil of material existence. These reflections (*anupreksha*) are engaged in regard to the following facts of human life:

1. Everything that the senses can possibly grasp is transitory.
2. Beings are utterly helpless in the face of certain death.
3. Every individual is trapped in the cycle of repeated incarnation into the finite world.
4. Each individual is completely alone in his or her experience of the ups and downs of the cycle of rebirth.

5. The spirit and the body are totally separate from each other.

6. Even the most attractive physical body is flawed and impure.

7. Human life is determined by the influx of karmic matter that, like cosmic dust, exists everywhere in the universe and that adheres to the spirit, or soul, which is filled with desire, obscuring each individual's inherent freedom.

8. The karmic influx can be stopped by means of the Jaina path.

9. Karmic matter presently adhering to the human spirit can be removed.

10. The universe is beginningless and without Creator, and therefore everyone is entirely responsible for his or her own salvation.

11. True insight (*bodhi*) is hard to attain, and human beings are in a privileged position to attain it.

12. The teachings of the *jinas,* the masters of Jainism, lead to ultimate liberation from the cycle of repeated existence and suffering.

The Jaina monk is encouraged to steadily dwell on these important doctrinal matters, until his understanding of them has become spontaneous. This practice enables him to cultivate equanimity in all circumstances, regardless how difficult or painful they may be. It also empowers him to patiently endure the many strict monastic disciplines and austerities like extensive fasting, standing in the midday sun, or sitting outside during cold weather. The purpose of these meditations and voluntary hardships is to strengthen the will as well as the monk's power of concentration. Only when he can check the flow of consciousness, preventing it from streaming out toward sense objects, is he able to move awareness to higher levels of existence until the spiritual essence (*jiva*) is realized. The spirit, or soul, has the three fundamental qualities of awareness, bliss, and energy, which define its existence beyond space and time.

THE TWELVE SIGNS OF THE ZODIAC

Astrology was an important aspect of spirituality in the ancient world. The sages and priests looked to the celestial forces for guidance in everyday matters concerning the people at large. Originally, astrology was purely descriptive divination. It was used to determine the auspicious and inauspicious moments in the life of a city-state or a nation. Often the life of the ruler or king, who represented the principles and laws of heaven on earth, served as the basis for the astrological predictions of the priests. Only much later, possibly with the Greeks, did astrology begin to be applied to the fate of ordinary individuals.

It is difficult to say when the zodiacal signs were first employed by astrologers. Some 4,000 years ago, the Babylonians worked with a list of eighteen constellations, which included ten of the twelve in use today. The twelvefold zodiac, divided into equal segments, is a far later invention, perhaps going back to 500 B.C. This symbolic configuration, which is reckoned on the basis of the equinoxes, is known as the tropical zodiac, as opposed to the sidereal zodiac of the actual constellations. The two zodiacs coincided roughly 2,000 years ago, but at this point are a sign apart. Thus if a person's sun sign is Aries, the sidereal sign is Pisces.

The twelve zodiacal constellations which have come down to us from the Chaldeans are: Aries, Taurus, Gemini, Cancer, Leo, Virgo, Libra, Scorpio, Sagittarius, Capricorn, Aquarius, and Pisces. The Chinese zodiac has the following equivalents: Rat, Ox, Tiger, Hare, Dragon, Snake, Horse, Sheep, Monkey, Fowl, Dog, and Pig. These zodiacal signs were looked upon as the heavenly mansions through which the seven known planets, the sun, and the moon traveled. Each planetary position along this celestial path, as well as the relationships between the planets and the two luminaries, was held to have significance for life on earth. The ancients also were very concerned about eclipses, comets, and other phenomena of the sky.

The wandering lights in the heavens were viewed as representing gods and goddesses, just as for untold eons the sun was venerated as a great spirit being, until modern science replaced this spiritual vision with a purely materialistic explanation. The cosmic interactions between the planets and luminaries were believed to hold tremendous importance for all mortals. Above all, the archetypal pattern created by these celestial entities served as an example to be emulated here on earth.

The astral deities dictated when temples, palaces, or other public structures were to be erected, important ceremonies to be held, or when seasonal planting was to occur. "As above, so below": This maxim was fundamental to ancient morality. According to Schwaller de Lubicz, the Alsatian scholar who pioneered the symbolic interpretation of ancient Egypt's artifacts, the same hermetic principle is mathematically codified in the curiously asymmetric

Temple of Luxor in Egypt. He has shown that the strange alignments of this vast structure are no accident but a deliberate and sophisticated creation. The temple is a symbolic representation of the idealized human being, who reflects the mathematics of the heavens.

A standing human body can be superimposed on the temple in such a way that chambers, colonnades, walls, and inscriptions correspond to various vital anatomical parts. The esoteric knowledge and symbolism embodied in the temple complex was not completely lost, for some manuscripts have reached us from medieval Christian times which assign the zodiacal animals to specific parts of the human body.

THE TWELVE TRIBES OF ISRAEL

Whenever the ancient Israelites set up camp during their forty years of wandering through the wilderness, they always formed a square, with the sacred tabernacle in the center. In clockwise order, the following three tribes camped to the south of the holy of holies: Reuben, Simeon, and Gad; to the west were Ephraim, Manasseh, and Benjamin; to the north were Dan, Asher, and Naphtali; and to the east were Judah, Issachar, and Zebulun. Sometimes the Manasseh and Ephraim are counted as one tribe, and in some lists the priestly Levi tribe is included.

According to tradition, the encampment pattern was based on the zodiac, though exactly which tribe was associated with which sign is not known. Their emblems were (in the same order as above): the rising sun, a tower, a tent, a bull, a palm tree, a wolf, a serpent, an olive tree, a doe, a lion cub, a donkey, and a ship. When the tribes finally crossed the river Jordan from east to west, arriving in Canaan, they placed twelve commemorative stones on Mount Ebal.

The Israelites were by no means alone in this twelve-fold organization. The Arameans and Edomites favored the same arrangement. Later the Saracens and Nabataeans followed the same twelvefold division. Twelve was a favored number in biblical times, and in many cases may have had a zodiacal derivation or significance.

After the prosperous reign of King Solomon, the unity between the tribes was progressively undermined. The ten tribes of the kingdom of Israel that occupied the northern territory split from the southern kingdom of Judah and Benjamin. In 722 B.C., the ten northern tribes were conquered and deported by the Assyrians, and their destiny remains a mystery. Speculations are rife, and the lost tribes have been identified with the American Indian tribes and the Mayas. There are traditionalist Jews who are still waiting for the fulfillment of Ezekiel's prophecy that the lost tribes will one day return to their homeland.

Within Christianity, it was St. John whose vision, as described in the Book of Revelation, revealed the New Jerusalem to be a twelve-gated city inhabited by twelve tribes. The twelve gates were guarded by as many angels, and there were twelve foundations to the city wall, each wall bearing the name of one of the twelve apostles of Jesus. In the center of the city was the tree of life, which has twelve kinds of fruit. Here we have archaic symbolism, which is found also in other cultures and spiritual traditions. At the root of it is the age-old division of the sun's path into twelve meaning-charged segments—the zodiac.

THE TWELVE SHIELDS OF THE
AMERICAN PLAINS INDIANS

The Plains Indians, comprising the Cheyenne, the Crow, and the Sioux, dwelled in the large area between the Mississipi river and the Rocky Mountains, and from central Texas to the Saskatchewan River in Canada. Religion played an important role in their lives, and both men and women actively sought contact with the spirit realm through vision quests and dreams.

Their most important spiritual ritual was the sun dance, celebrated annually in the summer. The dance was conducted around a tall painted pole fashioned from the wood of a sacred tree. The dancers moved around the pole for hours and even days, without taking either food or drink. In some tribes, the participants hung suspended from the pole, with skewers inserted into their chests. They whirled around until the skewers ripped through their skin. The goal was to achieve visions.

Their spiritual tradition knew of twelve sacred shields of light, which represented the twelve peoples of the world. Two of these peoples were the Indians themselves. These shields were passed from tribe to tribe where they were guarded by a special keeper, who could be a man or a woman. The shields were placed together at the time of annual renewal when they were stacked inside the twelve forked poles of the sun dance lodge.

The Plains Indians also had personal shields, and shields for men, women, and children, as well as forty-four peace shields. They were made from hides of bears, buffalos, deer, antelopes, or coyote, and so on. They were decorated with eagle plumes and fur tassels and painted with a variety of designs and symbols. They were not meant to be used in warfare and could be easily penetrated by an arrow.

Each shield was thought of as having special power, being a doorway to the spirit world. The twelve sacred shields, whose origin is lost in the remote past, evince the Plains Indians' philosophy of kinship with all beings.

THE TWELVE APOSTLES OF CHRISTIANITY

According to the New Testament, Jesus of Nazareth had twelve main disciples. St. Matthew gives their names as Simon Peter, Andrew, James, John, Philip, Bartholomew, Thomas, Matthew, James the son of Alphaeus, Thaddaeus, Simon the Canaanite, and Judas Iscariot. These men were personally chosen by Jesus, and they were the first bearers of his revelation. With the exception of Judas, they also were witnesses of his resurrection. According to St. Matthew's testimony, Judas hanged himself shortly after his betrayal of Jesus and so never even witnessed his master's crucifixion.

The number twelve has prompted all kinds of speculations. It echoes the twelve tribes of Israel. Possibly the twelve apostles were considered symbolic of the nucleus of the new Israel that honored and welcomed Jesus as the Messiah, or Christ. After Judas' death, Matthias was placed in the position of the twelfth disciple.

The number twelve stands for completion, which is most obvious in the symbolism of the zodiac. In early Christianity, the Christ was clearly associated with the sun. Some Gnostics, who were inspired by the Egyptian mystery tradition, hailed him as the new Amun. This solar symbolism has been preserved in the Western hermetic tradition. In view of this linkage of the Christ with solar symbolism, we may be justified in connecting the apostles with the twelve zodiacal signs.

This is borne out, for instance, by the depiction of a twelve-rayed sun in the basilica of San Miniato al Monte, in Florence, which is a thirteenth-century church full of arcane astrological symbolism. The medieval monks Christianized the zodiac, renaming it the "Crown or the Circle of the Holy Apostles" (*corona seu circulus sanctorum apostolorum*). In other words, Jesus and his core followers were viewed as cosmic representations, which fits the picture we have of early spiritual traditions.

THE TWELVE IMAMS OF ISLAM

Among the Sunnis, the predominant denomination within Islam, the leader of prayers at the mosque is called *imam,* which means literally "he who stands before" in the sense of "model" or "exemplar." In the Shi'ite minority denomination, the "imam" is a title reserved for the highest spiritual leader. His authority is said to derive directly from the prophet Muhammad through a line of succession among the descendants of Ali, Muhammad's cousin and son-in-law. Like the Christian pope, the imam is infallible. For the Sunnis, infallibility is true only of the prophet himself.

Every era is said to have its own imam, though he may not always make himself known, since in the past imams have been threatened with violence. The Shi'ite sect of the Twelvers recognizes twelve such imams, each succeeding imam having been appointed by his predecessor. The twelve imams are:

1. 'Ali ibn Abi Talib (598–661 A.D.);

2. al-Husayn (624–680 A.D.), the second son of 'Ali, who was killed by the soldiers of Yazid, the second Umayyad caliph, and became an instant symbol of martyrdom for the Shi'ite Muslims;

3. al-Hasan (625–670 A.D.), the son of 'Ali;

4. 'Ali ibn al-Husayn (died c. 712 A.D.), the son of al-Husayn;

5. Muhammad al-Baqir (died 731 A.D.);

6. Ja'far al-Sadiq (669–765 A.D.), who happened to be an adept in the arcane sciences, including alchemy, was largely responsible for the transformation of Shi'ism from a religious movement with a distinctly political flavor to a spiritual tradition;

7. Musa al-Kazim (died 799 A.D.);

8. Ali al-Rida (died 818 A.D.);

9. Muhammad al-Jawad (died 835 A.D.);

10. Ali al-Hadi (died 818 A.D.);

11. al-Hasan al-'Askari (died 874 A.D.);

12. Muhammad al-Mahdi, who entered into seclusion in 940 A.D. and is expected to return one day from what is known as his self-chosen "occultation," or concealment.

The twelfth imam was reputedly born in 869 A.D. in Samarra and disappeared at the age of four shortly after the death of his father, the eleventh imam. For about sixty years after his disappearance, he apparently made his will known through representatives. Since that time, known as the "lesser occultation," there has been total silence. He is said to have been hidden from the world, without the possibility of his discovery, but is expected to return as the Mahdi ("Guided One"). He is also named the "Awaited Mahdi" and the "Lord of the Age." His return signals the end of the world and the Day of Judgment.

According to the Shi'ites, one cannot be saved without following the imam, who is credited with supernatural knowledge (*'ilm*) and spiritual authority (*nass*). He acts as an intermediary between the faithful Muslim and God. The Shi'ites regard pilgrimage to the tombs of the imams and the annual commemoration of Husayn's martyrdom as important spiritual practices. Like the Hindu *avataras* or "divine descents," the imams of Shi'ism are seen as visible proof of God's presence in the world. They are the "gate to God" (*bab Allah*).

THE TWELVE PROPHETS OF THE JUDEO–CHRISTIAN TRADITION

The Greek word *prophet* means "one who speaks for another." The Hebrew word used in the Old Testament is *nabi'*. A prophet is the mouthpiece for, or messenger of, God. Moses is the archetype of the biblical prophet. The Bible also has a Greek name for a lesser prophet whose message is of doubtful authenticity: *mantis*.

Prophets appear in many spiritual traditions, notably Judaism, Christianity, and Islam. In ancient Mesopotamia, the temple priests were also ecstatic oracles, or prophets. Their prophecies had to do with the fate of king and country. These prophet-priests were both respected and feared. Later in history, as in classical Greece, oracles were also consulted by private individuals, the Delphic oracle being the most famous.

The early Israelites shared with the other cultures of the Mediterranean a certain flair for ecstatic states in which a "seer" would penetrate the curtain of tangible existence and behold what was hidden from the eyes of ordinary mortals. Although a seer's or prophet's oracular utterances were listened to with eagerness or apprehension, as the case may be, the soothsayer himself was often looked at as a madcap. No less a Hebrew prophet than Jeremiah warned against prophets, diviners, dreamers, enchanters, and sorcerers, who enthralled their credulous audiences with lies about Yahweh's intentions.

Within Judaism, a new, "literary" tradition of prophecy is thought to have begun with Amos about the middle of the eighth century B.C. He was followed by such respected prophets as Isaiah, Jeremiah, and Ezekiel, who are the three "major" prophets according to Judaism.

Both Judaism and Christianity agree on the identity of the twelve "minor" prophets: Hosea, Joel, Amos, Obadiah, Jonah, Micah, Nahum, Habakkuk, Zephaniah, Haggai, Zechariah, and Malachi. Apart from the Book of Jonah, which is biographical, the other writings are collections of sayings by the prophets, but also include materials from later times.

~13~

THE THIRTEEN ORIGINAL CLAN MOTHERS
IN THE NATIVE AMERICAN TRADITION

One of the sacred obligations in the Native American tradition is to feel kinship with all beings, including one's ancestors. Indeed, respecting the elders—whether alive or passed over—and listening to their wisdom is an integral part of the Native American heritage.

The Kiowa people, one of the tribes of the Plains Indians, have an ancient legend that tells of thirteen original clan mothers, who were the wisdom keepers. Long ago, after the world's destruction by fire, they assumed adult human bodies, walked the earth for a while, taught other women, and then mysteriously vanished again, leaving behind thirteen crystal skulls. The clan mothers are the healing aspect of Grandmother Moon and Mother Earth.

Each clan mother created a medicine shield that epitomized her specific gifts. These shields can be used as props for meditation to get in touch with the spiritual essence of one or the other clan mother. The shields contain the original "medicine" that they brought into the world. The thirteen clan mothers are:

1. Talks with Relations, who is the mother of Nature, the guardian of weather and the seasons;

2. Wisdom Keeper, who is the historian of events on earth and protectress of the sacred traditions;

3. Weighs the Truth, who is the teacher of divine law and guardian of justice;

4. Looks Far Woman, who is the prophetess and door-keeper of the path to illumination;

5. Listening Woman, who is the teacher of silence and introspection;

6. Storyteller, who is the teacher of faith, humility, and innocence;

7. Loves All Things, who is the keeper of unconditional love and sexual wisdom;

8. She Who Heals, who is the keeper of the healing arts, rites of passage, and the mysteries of life and death;

9. Setting Sun Woman, who is the keeper of hopes and goals and the guardian of unborn generations;

10. Weaves the Web, who is the guardian of all creativity as well as the destructive principle;

11. Walks Tall Woman, who is the teacher of integrity, persistence, and self-esteem and the guardian of leadership and new pathways;

12. Gives Praise, who is the mother of abundance and the keeper of ritual, ceremony, and magic;

13. Becomes Her Vision, who is the guardian of cycles of transformation and spiritual evolution.

In her book *The Thirteen Clan Mothers,* Jamie Sams, a Kiowa Indian, sums up this wise oral tradition in the following words: "My Elders told me that every human being is connected to the Thirteen Original Clan Mothers and that when a person is ready for that level of spiritual experience, the dreams of the Crystal Skulls, the Whirling Rainbow, or the Clan Mothers will come to them."

THE THIRTEEN CARDINAL TENETS OF JUDAISM

The Jews have traditionally been more strict about religious practice than about belief, tolerating a considerable spectrum of philosophical opinions. For a long time no effort was made to organize the rabbinic traditions into a coherent theology. It was primarily under the influence of Christianity and Islam that Jewish intellectuals developed a formal theology.

Foremost among them was Moses ben Maimon (1135–1204 A.D.), better known as Maimonides and sometimes called the "second Moses." Apart from writing medical treatises, he was the author of the widely studied *Guide for the Perplexed,* which was originally written in Arabic and subsequently translated into Hebrew and Latin. In this work he labored to show that philosophy and religion were essentially compatible endeavors. In his monumental *Mishnah Torah* he offered an unsurpassed systematization of rabbinical law and ritual. Among other things, Maimonides formulated the commonly accepted list of Jewish doctrines. The thirteen principles of faith are:

1. The existence of God;
2. The unique unity of God, which is a oneness unlike any other;

3. God has no material being, and all biblical references to parts of God's body must be understood purely metaphorically;

4. God is eternal;

5. God alone deserves to be worshipped;

6. The words of the prophets are messages from God;

7. Moses was the greatest of the prophets, and he alone received God's word in full consciousness;

8. Moses received the entire Torah directly from God;

9. Nothing may ever be added or omitted from the Torah;

10. God is aware of all human behavior;

11. After death, God rewards the good and punishes the wicked;

12. God will send the Messiah;

13. Upon the coming of the Messiah, the dead will be resurrected in bodily form.

The last doctrinal principle, which Maimonides had added as an afterthought, caused widespread controversy, even though the idea of resurrection had been in circulation since rabbinic times.

~14~

THE FOURTEEN STATIONS OF THE CROSS

The fourteen Stations of the Cross, also called the Way of the Cross, is a devotional practice in Catholicism and in many Anglican churches that commemorates Jesus' last journey from the house of Pilate to Calvary and from there to the tomb. This popular practice consists of a prayer and short meditation before each of the fourteen representations of the Christ. This ritual was started in the mid-fourteenth century, and probably derived from the earlier tradition of pilgrimage to the Holy Land. It may have received an extra impetus from returning Crusaders who had walked the way of the cross in Jerusalem.

At first, the number of stations varied from five to thirty, and also the theme of each was not fixed. The series of fourteen stations became popular in the sixteenth century and was formalized by Pope Clement XII in 1731. More recently, a fifteenth station is sometimes added, recollecting the moment of resurrection.

The fourteen stations are most often arranged around the inner walls of a church but may also be found outside in the church grounds, especially on hills. The fourteen stations are:

1. Jesus is sentenced to death.
2. Jesus is laden with the cross.
3. Jesus stumbles and falls with the cross on his shoulder.
4. Jesus meets his mother.
5. Simon of Cyrene helps Jesus carry the cross.
6. Veronica wipes Jesus' face with her veil.
7. Jesus falls a second time.
8. Jesus comforts the women of Jerusalem.
9. Jesus falls a third time.
10. Jesus is stripped of his garments.
11. Jesus is nailed to the cross.
12. Jesus dies.
13. Jesus is taken down from the cross and placed in Mary's arms.
14. Jesus' body is laid in the tomb.

These fourteen incidents are used by the faithful to recollect as vividly as possible the suffering of the Christ, who is said to have died for the sins of all. The ritual can be done privately or more formally, with a priest present.

THE FOURTEEN LEVELS OF SPIRITUAL COMPETENCE IN JAINISM

Jainism speaks of five causes of bondage to the material realm, namely false vision, lack of restraint, inattention, passion, and activity. The spiritual path is a progressive liberation of the human soul from these qualities. Jainism recognizes fourteen levels or stages of spiritual qualification, known as the *guna-sthanas*. They are:

1. The level of false vision (*mithya-drishti*), which is the lowest developmental stage of the human soul. It is the result of spiritual ignorance and the presence of the passions, which effectively trap the individual in the cycle of repeated births and deaths. At the upper end of this level, the practitioner is called an *apunar-bandhaka,* or one who endeavors not to remain bound and who seeks to cultivate true wisdom.

2. The level of mixed taste (*sasvadana*), which is reached only when the individual falls from a higher level of spiritual development due to the reappearance of deluding karmas or passions.

3. The level of true deludedness (*samyag-mithyatva*), which is a transitional stage in which true vision is mixed with false beliefs, causing the mind to waver between reality and illusion.

4. The level of true vision (*samyag-drishti*), which is the first step on the path of liberation, where the individual is firmly convinced of the limitations of his or her previous notions about reality and is wholeheartedly committed to spiritual life.

5. The level of partial restraint (*desha-virata*), which is attained through practicing the vows prescribed for a lay person. Dissoluteness (*avirati*) is partially overcome.

6. The level of total restraint (*sarva-virata*), which calls for the practice of the great vows prescribed for ascetics. At this stage, passion is fully overcome. However, there is still a certain inattention (*pramada*), which must be mastered.

7. The level of restraint free from inattention (*apramatta-virata*), which is achieved through intensive meditation (*dhyana*).

8. The level of the new exercise (*apurva-karana*), in which the intensity and duration of karmas are greatly reduced through the practice of intensely blissful meditation.

9. The level of the exercise of non–return (*anivritti-karana*), which is a profound meditative state.

10. The level of subtle warding-off (*sukshma-samparaya*), which is a still more profound meditation, leading to the elimination of the subtle forms of karma and delusion. Levels 8 through 10 are called the "ladder" (*shreni*), which the practitioner ascends in order to either temporarily suppress or actually eliminate the karmic conditioning.

11. The level of appeased delusion (*upashanta-moha*), which is attained by merely tranquilizing the "flaming" passions temporarily. To make proper progress, the aspirant must eliminate the passions completely; otherwise there is the danger of falling back into lower stages of practice.

12. The level of eliminated delusion (*kshina-moha*), which coincides with the transcendence of the passions even in their subtle form as delusive karma (*mohaniya-karma*). Further spiritual growth is now inevitable.

13. The level of omniscience associated with activity (*sayoga-kevalin*), which eliminates all remaining karma and brings omniscience (*kevala-jnana*). The Sanskrit word *kevalin* means literally "alone," which is the state of the spirit's perfect isolation from matter. However, the liberated spirit (*jiva*) is not a windowless monad but is deemed to know all things—past, present, and future. *Kevalin* is shorthand for *kevala-jnana,* or omniscience.

14. The level of omniscience without activity (*ayoga-kevalin*), which is attained just prior to death when all activity (*yoga*) ceases.

Finally, there is liberation (*moksha*), which is not considered a level of spiritual unfolding but the condition of the spirit when it is not encumbered by ignorance and karma. The liberated adept (*siddha*) is mere spirit, and as such interpenetrates all the other countless spirits. However, it is generally held that in our age of spiritual darkness, lay practitioners and also ascetics (monks and nuns) cannot progress beyond the fifth and sixth level respectively.

~18~

THE EIGHTEEN BLESSINGS IN JUDAISM

A blessing is a declaration of divine praise, which is used for God ("Blessed be the Lord") but also for fellow humans and natural objects or phenomena. In the latter case, the blessing is likewise a reminder of the omnipresent blessedness of the Divine.

The Hebrew term for it is *barak,* which is derived from the root *brk* from which also the word for "knee" is formed. The historical reason for this is that the ancient Hebrews knelt for their worship and to receive the blessings of Yahweh. Formal blessings in liturgical contexts are called benedictions. They play an important role in both Judaism and Christianity.

In the second century A.D., Rabbi Meir decreed that a Jew should recite one hundred blessings every day. One of the tractates of the Talmud bears the title *Berakoth,* meaning "Blessings." It is a compendium of prayers intended as blessings, or thanksgivings. In the twelfth century A.D., Moses Maimonides spoke of three categories of blessing: blessings for enjoyment, which are proffered before and after meals, or before inhaling the scent of spices or perfumes; blessings associated with the performance of a commandment; and blessings of gratitude in the face of witnessing the wonders of Nature, such as sunrise, lightning, or comets.

According to a systematization that appears to have been made at the time of the Second Temple (first century A.D.), there are eighteen blessings, which were later edited by Rabban Gamaliel II. They are also known as "the Eighteen" (*Shemoneh-Esreh*), and are used in the *amidah* ("standing"), the prescribed daily prayer. These blessings are all addressed to God as declarations of praise and gratitude. They acknowledge God's greatness, holiness, love, healing power, and redeeming spirit.

These blessings are intended to serve as a vivid reminder of the presence of God in this world and of our human dependence on him: God is the source of all blessings.

THE TWENTY-FOUR FORD-MAKERS OF JAINISM

Vardhamana Mahavira, an older contemporary of the Buddha, was the last of the "ford-makers" (*tirthankara*) of the Jaina tradition. They are so called because they prepare a bridge across the ocean of conditioned existence and suffering which leads others safely to liberation. He was not the actual founder of Jainism, but a reanimator of ancient wisdom.

The Jainas venerate the semi-legendary Rishabha as the original founder of Jainism. He is thought to have lived in Vedic times, because the name Rishabha is mentioned in several hymns of the *Rig-Veda*. According to traditional Hindu sources, which are slowly being confirmed by modern scholarship, the oldest of the Vedic hymns reflect knowledge of an era that may reach back well over six thousand years.

He was followed by Ajita, Sambhava, Abhinandana, Sumati, Padmaprabha, Suparshva, Candraprabha, Suvidhi Pushpadanta, Shitala, Shreyamsha, Vasupujya, Vimala, Ananta, Dharma, Shanti, Kunthu, Ara, Malli (the only female ford-maker), and Munisuvrata, whose lives are a total enigma.

Nami, the twenty-second ford-maker, lived in Saurashtra and is sometimes thought to have been a contemporary of Krishna, the God-man venerated in Vaishnavism and the *Bhagavad-Gita*. Following traditional Hindu chronology, this would place him around 3100 B.C.

He was followed by Arishtanemi, who supposedly was the son of King Samudravijaya, a brother of Vasudeva (the father of Krishna).

Then came Parshva, who is thought to have lived in the middle of the ninth century B.C. in the region of the holy city of Benares in Northern India. At the end of this illustrious lineage of twenty-three great liberated teachers, or spiritual "conquerors" (*jinas*), appeared Mahavira, who was probably born in 599 B.C. and lived just over seventy years. They all served their followers as inspiring examples and guides on the path to liberation. Jaina temples contain statues of the twenty-four tirthankaras, which are viewed as focal points of their spiritual energy.

THE TWENTY-FOUR PRINCIPLES
OF EXISTENCE IN SAMKHYA

In its classic form, the Samkhya ("Enumeration") school of Hinduism recognizes twenty-four categories of existence belonging to the realm of Nature (*prakriti*). The twenty-fifth principle, which lies utterly beyond Nature, is the Self (*purusha*).

The Self is defined by the Samkhya thinkers as the eternal pure witness of Nature's activities. It is the principle of consciousness. There are many such Selves, which are all omniscient and omnipresent (and hence interpenetrating on the transcendental level). They provide the light of consciousness for the finite body-minds with which they are somehow associated. The body-minds of beings have no consciousness in themselves, because Nature is regarded as completely insentient. Even the highest evolved category within Nature, the suprapersonal mind (*buddhi*) has no light of its own, but is like the moon that merely reflects the luminosity of the sun.

The alpha and omega of the Samkhya path is the eternal Self, which is realized through a person's progressive disidentification with, and deep renunciation of, all the various aspects and levels of Nature. To assist the spiritual aspirant in this task, the Samkhya sages have charted the hierarchical realms of Nature. The following are the twenty-four categories or principles of existence, called *tattvas*:

1. The transcendental ground of Nature, or *prakriti-pradhana,* which is the origin of all finite objects, whether material or immaterial.

2. The transpersonal mind (*buddhi*), which is the organ of higher wisdom transcending the ego.

3. The principle of individuation, known as the "I-maker" (*ahamkara*), which gives rise to the remaining evolutes.

4. The lower mind (*manas*), which processes the sensory input.

5–9. The five sense capacities (*jnana-indriya*), namely seeing, hearing, touching, tasting, and smelling.

10–14. The five actions capacities (*karma-indriya*), namely speaking, grasping, walking, excreting, and procreating.

15–19. The five sensory potentials (*tanmatra*), namely sound, touch, form, taste, and smell.

20–24. The five material elements (*bhuta*).

Through meditation, the aspirant withdraws attention from the material world and the sensory potentials, and he or she disables temporarily the five sense capacities and five action capacities. Next the chatter of the lower mind must be completely conquered, so that the sense of identity is located in the higher mind (buddhi). Even the alluring activities of the higher mind—wisdom and all kinds of paranormal powers—must not detain the aspirant. He or she must press on to the transcendental ground of Nature itself, but even this advanced state of spiritual realization must not be confused with genuine Self-realization. Those who commit this error are known as *prakriti-layas,* or those who have become absorbed in the world-ground. They are capable of shifting shape at will, and their lifespan is extraordinarily long, lasting for an entire world age. Yet, they are not truly liberated.

The remaining spiritual task is to exercise both utmost discernment (*viveka*) and dispassion (*vairagya*). In that elevated, God-like state, the adept must be willing to give up everything so that he or she may recover the transcendental Self in its sheer simplicity. The adept must realize beyond any shadow of doubt that consciousness is extraneous to Nature, and that consciousness is one's true identity. Only then occurs the radical shift from conditioned existence to liberation (*kaivalya*).

~32~

THE THIRTY-TWO SECRET PATHS
IN THE KABBALAH

The thirty-two secret paths of wisdom known to Kabbalists are formed of the twenty-two connecting lines between the ten *sefiroth* of the Kabbalah and the ten sefiroth themselves. Together they are considered the matrices of the universe. The number 32 symbolizes totality: the wholeness of all actual and potential phenomena.

Each of the connecting lines between the ten sefiroth is associated with a particular letter of the Hebrew alphabet, which has twenty-two letters in all. The Hebrew alphabet is thought to be charged with deep esoteric significance and numinous power. Each letter not only has a particular shape and sound but also a corresponding numeric value. For instance, the letter *aleph* equals 1, *beth* equals 2, *yod* equals 10, and final *tzadde* equals 900. Thus the divine name Yahweh (YHWH), which must never be pronounced, is given the numeric value of 26.

This number also is ascribed to the secret path between *tifaret* ("beauty") and *hod* (splendor). In the sefirotic tree of life, tifaret occupies the center, and on the physical level, corresponds both to the sun and the human heart.

Hod, which is presided over by the Archangel Michael, corresponds to the planet Mercury and the color yellow. It also is associated with the act of submission, which is a form of dependence on a higher reality without however sacrificing individuality, or personal integrity.

The thirty-two aspects of the Kabbalistic tree of life represent specific ways of approaching the Divine, or states of consciousness. These bear the following names: mystical (*mufla*); radiant (*maz'hir*); sanctified (*mekudash*); settled (*kavua*); rooted (*nishrash*); transcendental influx (*shefa nivdal*); hidden (*nistar*); perfect (*shalem*); pure (*tahor*); scintillating (*mitnotzetz*); glaring (*metzuchtzach*); glowing (*bahir*); unity directing (*manhig haachdut*); illuminating (*meir*); stabilizing (*ma'amid*); enduring (*nitzchi*); sensory (*hahergesh*); house of influx (*bet hashefa*); mystery of all spiritual activities (*sod hapaulot haruchniot kulam*); will (*haratzon*); desired and sought (*hachafutz vehamevukash*); faithful (*ne'eman*); sustaining (*kayam*); apparitive (*dimyoni*); testing (*nisyoni*); renewing (*mechudash*); palpable (*murgash*); natural (*mutba*); physical (*mugsham*); general (*kelali*); continuous (*tamidi*); and worshipped consciousness (*ne'evad sekhel*).

The Jewish mystic aspires to union (*devekut*, literally "cleaving") with God through communion with his various emanations (the ten sefiroth). However, this union is never a complete merging, as is the case of most schools of Hindu esotericism. For the Kabbalist, there is an eternal abyss between the Creator and his creatures—a gulf that is lessened but never entirely bridged by mystical ecstasy.

THE THIRTY-TWO MARKS OF A BUDDHA

The ancient traditions held that the divine order should be duplicated in the world. This idea naturally led to the belief that the perfected beings—those who are faithfully mirroring the celestial harmony in their own life—have special bodily signs by which they can be recognized.

Thus the Mahayana Buddhist scriptures mention the thirty-two marks (*lakshana*) of a Buddha: (1) a protuberance on the skull, called *ushnisha*; (2) glossy black hair with short curls turning from left to right; (3) a broad, smooth brow; (4) a small ball-like protuberance (*urna*) or a tuft of silvery hair between the eyebrows; (5) large eyelashes; (6) brilliant black eyes; (7) forty perfectly even teeth, (8) that lie close together and (9) are dazzlingly white; (10) a mellifluous voice; (11) a large, long tongue; (12) refined sense of taste; (13) jaws like those of a lion; (14) round shoulders and arms; (15) the seven parts of the body are round and full; (16) the space between the shoulders is filled out; (17) a golden-hued skin; (18) long arms that reach down to the knees; (19) a strong upper torso like that of a lion; (20) a figure resembling a banyan tree; (21) only a single hair grows from each pore and (22) curl to the right; (23) the genitals are hidden; (24) round thighs; (25) gazelle-like legs; (26) long fingers and nails; (27) elongated heels; (28) a high instep; (29) slender and delicate hands and feet; (30) webbing between fingers and toes; (31) a shining, thousand-spoked wheel on each sole, and (32) flat feet that are firmly planted on the ground.

Some Buddhist texts also list eighty inferior marks. Clearly, all these physical attributes of the "great man" (*maha-purusha*) are idealizations that can hardly be expected to correspond to historical reality but serve as guidelines for artistic depictions of the Buddha.

THE FORTY HOURS OF JESUS IN THE TOMB

According to the Gospel of Mark, which is thought to be the earliest of the gospels, Jesus died on the cross around three o'clock on a Friday afternoon. In the evening of Jesus' crucifixion, one of his wealthy disciples, a man named Joseph of Arimathea, claimed the body. He laid Jesus' body in his own new tomb and sealed off the tomb's entrance with a heavy stone. Remembering that the troublemaker Jesus had prophesied his resurrection after three days, the chief priests and the Pharisees insisted that the Roman procurator Pontius Pilate post an armed guard in front of the tomb. They wanted to make sure that none of Jesus' followers would surreptitiously remove the body and then claim Jesus had risen from the dead.

We learn from the Gospel of Matthew that when Mary Magdalene and Mary the mother of James visited the tomb two days later, an angel came in an earthquake and rolled aside the huge stone covering the tomb. The angel announced to the two women that Jesus had been raised from the dead and was on his way to Galilee where they could see him. The Gospel of Mark informs us that all this happened early in the morning, "when the sun had risen." However, St. John in his gospel claims that it was still dark.

When the priests heard the news, they bribed the soldiers to claim that Jesus' disciples had come by night and stolen the body. In this way they hoped to discredit the Christians and silence any talk about Jesus' resurrection.

Jesus must have risen by seven o'clock in the morning of the second day after his crucifixion, for there is an old tradition that he spent forty hours in the tomb. This period is commemorated in the ceremony of the "Forty Hours Devotion" in the Roman Catholic Church.

Whether or not Jesus actually was in the tomb for that exact length of time is impossible to say. Perhaps the forty hours were meant to have a purely symbolic value, since forty is a favored number in the Old Testament as well as the New Testament. Thus tradition has it that the flood lasted for forty days; the Israelites wandered for forty years in the Sinai desert; Moses spent forty days on the mountain talking with God; Jesus fasted in the desert for forty days; Solomon, David, and several other kings ruled for forty years, and so on. Judging from most of the biblical references, the number forty suggests a period of preparation or maturation.

Regardless of the historicity of the gospel accounts of Jesus' burial, belief in his resurrection is pivotal to Christianity. Christian and non-Christian researchers continue to puzzle over the enigma of the last days of Jesus. Ever-new theories are put forward, including the claim that Jesus went to Kashmir after his resurrection. There is, in fact, a very old but still unauthenticated local tradition that identifies a certain saintly person by the name of Yuz Asaf with Jesus and that speaks of Jesus' final burial in a tomb in the city of Srinigar in the Himalayas.

~ 64 ~

THE SIXTY-FOUR YOGINIS OF TANTRISM

Tantrism revolves around the celebration of the feminine principle (*shakti*) in its various forms—from the Mother Goddess to the *kundalini* ("serpent power") within the body, to the minor female deities responsible for certain worldly or spiritual functions, to the female participants in the sexual ritual of left-hand Tantrism.

The Sanskrit word *yogini* is the feminine form of the noun *yogi* (or *yogin*), which denotes a practitioner of Yoga. The word *yoga* itself means both "union" and "discipline." Thus, in an ordinary context, a yogini is simply a female practitioner of the unitive discipline of Yoga. In left-hand Tantrism, the term refers to the consecrated sexual partner of a yogi who seeks to find the great bliss (*ananda*) through the spiritual transmutation of the biological urge.

However, in right-hand Tantrism, which understands the sexual ritual in purely metaphoric terms, the yogini is not a flesh-and-blood woman but the internalized "sex" partner: the Goddess herself. By worshipping the Goddess through complex visualization, breath control, and external rituals, the yogi awakens the kundalini force that slumbers at the lower pole of the bodily axis (the psychospiritual vortex at the base of the spine). The kundalini is a form of the Goddess herself. When that force is conducted upward to the topmost psychoenergetic center at the crown of the head, a state of mystical union is achieved. This state is conceptualized (and experienced) as the blissful marriage between God and Goddess.

All these various meanings of yogini are merged in the concept of the sixty-four yoginis, which are understood to be aspects of the great Goddess Durga ("Far-Going"). Their cultic worship emerged in the ninth century A.D., in Northern India. The sixty-four—or, according to some traditions, eight or sixteen—yoginis are minor deities or spirits who acquired their spiritual status through the magical power of Yoga and who are invoked, primarily but not exclusively, to facilitate the yogic process. They are viewed as sorceresses that embody the qualities of Durga, who is the Goddess of Tantrism par excellence. When the yogi succeeds in gaining the favor of one or all of these yoginis, he is assured of Durga's grace.

SEE ALSO The Ten Forms of the Goddess in Tantrism

~ 84 ~

THE EIGHTY–FOUR ADEPTS OF TANTRISM

Tantrism, whether Hindu or Buddhist, is a spiritual path that seeks to combine perfection with power. Both perfection and power are expressed in the same Sanskrit word: *siddhi.* The accomplished adept who has attained spiritual perfection, or liberation, is known as a *siddha.* However, a siddha is not merely a person who has realized the identity of *nirvana* and *samsara,* or transcendental reality and conditional reality. Adepthood also implies the possession of the eight great psychic powers of Yoga, the *ashta-siddhis.*

Thus, the great adepts (*maha-siddha*) are not only remembered as illumined masters but also as formidable magicians capable of the most extraordinary feats. The Tantric tradition knows of eighty-four such beings, who lived in the period between 800 and 1200 A.D. Their names have been preserved in a Tibetan text called "The Legends of the Eighty-Four Great Adepts." This collection of stories reputedly goes back to an Indian Buddhist scholar, Abhaya Datta, who in the twelfth century A.D. orally transmitted it to a Tibetan monk, Mondub Sherab.

The stories that have been handed down about these personages reveal them to have been very colorful individuals who, in their endeavor to communicate the spiritual path, often availed themselves of quite unorthodox means. They generally were antiestablishment iconoclasts, denouncing hypocrisy, empty ritualism, the caste system, and mere abstract philosophy. These great adepts came from all walks of life and included kings and servants, priests and scholars, merchants and hunters—even a thief, a gambler, and a prostitute. Most of the siddhas were men, but there were also several female adepts. Regardless of their background or form of teaching, they all spoke with the authority of spiritual realization.

The most venerated maha-siddhas are Minapa (Matsyendra), Lui-pa, Saraha, Goraksha, Nagarjuna, Naropa, and Tilopa. The historicity of these individuals should not be doubted, though what we know of them is scarcely reliable. Over the centuries, countless legends have been woven around these figures, celebrating their attainment of liberation as well as their display of miraculous powers.

Their teachings have, unfortunately, only been imperfectly preserved. In addition to a handful of works of uncertain authenticity, there are numerous didactic songs (*doha*), which contain the essence of their philosophy, or rather, philosophies. The maha-siddhas were inspired by Tantrism and many of them taught the ideal of physical immortality in a transformed body. This teaching is known as *kaya-sadhana* or "body cultivation," which involves the awakening of the body's dormant spiritual power (*kundalini-shakti*).

The maha-siddhas became the focus of popular veneration in Northern India and the Himalayan countries. In Southern India a similar pantheon is recognized, composed of eighteen such adepts, notably Agastya, Tirumular, and Civavakkiyar. The Southern pantheon also includes individuals of Chinese, Singhalese, and even Egyptian origin.

The siddhas are immortals who have conquered the elements and dimensions of exsistence. According to the *Aryabhatiya*—a fourth-century treatise on astronomy— the siddhas dwell in Siddhapura ("Adepts City"), which is said to be located in a distant place where the sun rises when it sets in India. If this is understood in conventional geographical terms, Siddhapura would have to be an American city. However, it is clear from most other sources that the siddhas do not belong to the earth plane, although they can manifest here at will. They are masters of time and space.

~ 95 ~

THE NINETY-FIVE THESES OF
MARTIN LUTHER IN CHRISTIANITY

Martin Luther (1483–1546 A.D.) became an Augustinian monk at the age of twenty-two in order to find peace with God. He diligently observed all the duties of a Catholic monk—confession, prayer, devotion, good works—but quickly found himself in a desperate struggle and a state of alienation. It seemed that the harder he tried to follow the monastic path, the farther removed he felt from God. After eight years of struggle, Luther suddenly found himself responding deeply to St. Paul's teaching of "justification by faith." He realized that the Creator, out of his infinite love for creation, freely forgives the sins of humankind and that no amount of effort or work can earn that forgiveness. Rather, God's grace can be received by those who have faith.

A brilliant and daring theologian, who later translated the entire Bible into German, Luther used his formidable scholarship to attack what he perceived to be the faulty ways and corruption of the Catholic Church. In the course, he fathered the Reformation and founded Protestantism.

Luther's belief in the sufficiency of God's grace and human faith was the theological and existential basis underlying his defiant act of posting his Ninety-Five Theses on the doors of the castle church in Wittenberg on October 31, 1517. Yet, curiously, salvation by faith is nowhere mentioned in his Theses, which mark the beginning of the Reformation.

Rather, in his Theses, Luther specifically protested against the widespread custom among the Catholic clergy of selling "indulgences." These were slips of paper guaranteeing the purchaser the absolution of sins.

Luther vigorously challenged the belief that Christ, Mary, and the saints accumulated a surplus of merit that the Church could sell. He denied that the indulgences could absolve anyone from guilt, and that they were positively harmful, because they gave sinners a false sense of security. He also pointed out that the Pope had no jurisdiction over purgatory. The Theses implied a far-reaching questioning of the Church's customary ways of raising funds.

Within weeks, Luther became the focus of a controversy that shook all of Europe. In 1520, Pope Leo X branded Luther a heretic who was like "a wild boar in the Lord's vineyard." He granted Luther sixty days to recant. When Luther publicly burned the Pope's bull, he was formally excommunicated and friends had to shelter him for ten months to save his life.

Once he was back in public, Luther proved a prodigious preacher and writer. For him the Church was primarily a spiritual community, not an official hierarchy. Apart from wanting to end the sale of indulgences, he also fought for abolishing celibacy of the clergy, the cult of Mary and the saints, masses for the dead, pilgrimages, religious orders, and other Catholic institutions.

~ 101 ~

THE 101 CONDUITS OF THE LIFE FORCE IN VEDANTA

To the clairvoyant sight of the yogis of India, the subtle body appears like an oval field criss-crossed by countless filaments of light: the luminous currents of the life force (*prana*). The ancient *Brihadaranyaka-Upanishad,* which is a compilation of esoteric Hindu teachings of more than three thousand years ago, mentions that there are 101 such currents or "conduits" (*nadi*) through which the life force circulates in the subtle body. Each conduit terminates at a specific location within the network of energy that forms the subtle body. Some of these termination points correspond, on the physical level, to specific organs, such as the eyes, ears, nose, mouth, finger tips, and so on.

The number 101 is symbolic rather than empirical, standing for a large number of energy filaments. Some traditions mention 72,000 and even 350,000 nadis. From *Katha-Upanishad,* a Sanskrit scripture that is several centuries younger than the *Brihadaranyaka,* we learn that of the 101 energy channels, only one passes all the way to the crown of the head. It is said to lead to immortality.

Later Yoga texts, especially from the tradition of

Tantrism and Hatha-Yoga, single out three energy currents for special treatment: the *ida-,* the *pingala-,* and the *sushumna-nadi.* The former two are described as winding in helical fashion around the *sushumna,* which runs along the bodily axis from the lowest psychoenergetic center at the base of the spine to the highest psychoenergetic plexus at the top of the head. The *ida* ("comforting") channel is on the left, and the *pingala* ("tawny") channel is on the right. The former carries "cool" lunar energy, corresponding to the parasympathetic nervous system on the physical level, and the latter carries "warm" solar energy, corresponding to the sympathetic nervous system.

In Tantrism and Hatha-Yoga the principal task of the yogis is to arouse the *kundalini-shakti,* or serpent power, in the lowest psychoenergetic vortex. Once awakened, this psychospiritual force rushes upward. Through concentration, visualization, and breath control, its ascent can be properly guided. If it enters into the wrong nadi, the kundalini can cause tremendous damage to the subtle and physical structures. Its proper pathway is the central conduit, or *sushumna-nadi.* The yogis strive to remove all blockages from that channel, so that the serpent power can flow freely in it, reaching the topmost center (*cakra*) without doing damage to the body-mind.

According to medieval hatha-yoga manuals, the sushumna is composed of several layers—the *vajra* ("thunderbolt") *-nadi* within which is the *citrini* ("shining") *-nadi* within which is the *brahma-nadi.* The Sanskrit word *brahma* stands for the absolute nondual Reality itself.

Along the path of the sushumna are three major "knots" (*granthi*)—at the level of the heart, the throat, and the spot between the eyebrows (or, in some traditions, at the base of the spine). These knots, which are natural obstructions, must be pierced by the life force (prana), so that the full power of the *kundalini* energy can rush upward.

When the central conduit is fully activated through the arousal of the serpent power, sun and moon are said to stand still, together with time itself. What this means is that the solar and the lunar energy currents of the subtle body (and hence the two nervous systems) are temporarily transcended: The yogi enters the state of ecstatic unification (*samadhi*), experiencing the bliss of the Divine. For this reason, the "most gracious channel" or sushumna-nadi is also known as the "way of liberation" (*moksha-marga*).

SEE ALSO The Seven Psychospiritual Centers (Cakras) in Tantrism

~108~

THE 108 PILGRIMAGE CENTERS OF TANTRISM

In India, the number 108 is a sacred number, suggesting completeness or wholeness. Thus there are 108 sheperdesses (*gopi* devoted to Lord Krishna), 108 beads on the Hindu and Buddhist rosary, and there also are said to be 108 *Upanishads,* even though the actual number of these esoteric scriptures exceeds 200. The Buddhists know of 108 *arhats* or "worthy ones." This symbol–laden number has astronomical origins, it being the average distance of the moon from the earth in terms of the moon's diameter. The same ratio applies to the sun. However, in symbolism, the number 108 more specifically refers to the lunar principle. Curiously enough, the mineral silver, which traditionally represents the moon, has the atomic weight of 108. Not surprisingly, this number also has played an important role in the Kabbalah and the Western hermetic tradition as a whole.

According to the Tantric heritage, there are 108 pilgrimage centers (*pitha*) that are dedicated to the feminine (lunar) principle, or Shakti. There is a marvelous myth that explains the existence of these centers.

The Golden Age (known as the *krita-yuga* in Sanskrit) had passed, and a less perfect age was in motion.

God Shiva, heavenly prototype of ascetics and yogis, was constantly absorbed in deepest meditation. His austerities caused such heat that the universe was threatened with extinction. Brahma, the Creator, was understandably worried. He begged the Great Goddess to distract Shiva from his yogic efforts and engage him in love play, so that creation could continue to exist. The Mother of the Universe agreed to take human form in order to entrance Shiva, her beloved. She entered the womb of Virini, Daksha's wife, to be born as Sati ("She who is").

Sati was the first-born of the sixty daughters of Daksha. With the power of the Goddess within her, she succeeded in arousing Shiva's interest not only by her exquisite beauty but also by her asceticism. He asked her to be his wife and even assumed human form for her sake. When her father, Daksha, insulted Shiva at a feast, she entered into deep meditation and immolated herself.

Shiva, grief-stricken, recovered her partially consumed body from the flames of the sacrificial fire and bore it away into heaven. Fragments of her body fell to earth in 108 different places over the Indian subcontinent, filling each site with her holy presence. In time, these locations became places of Goddess worship (*devi-pitha*).

The three best known sites are the pithas near Calcutta, Kamakhya in Assam, and Jalandhara, which are said to be the locations of Sati's big toe, womb, and breast respectively. The womb (*yoni*), or female generative organ, has special significance in Tantrism, or Shaktism. It is the primary symbol of Shakti, the feminine power of the cosmos, which is responsible for all creativity.

Historically, the earliest Tantric scriptures mention only four pithas. Over time, these seem to have grown to first 51 (said to actually contain the relics of Sati) and later 108. Sati's self-immolation is the mythological core of the Hindu custom of suttee (from *sati*), where the widow enters the funeral pyre of her husband. This tradition was banned during the British rule in India.

~153~

THE 153 FISH IN CHRISTIANITY

Most Christians who have read the Bible are familiar with the story told in the Gospel of John of the miraculous catch of 153 fish, "caught in an unbroken net." After the crucifixion, Simon Peter and six other disciples of Jesus went fishing in the Sea of Tiberias (Galilee). Although they spent all night on the sea, they caught not a single fish. In the morning, a man—the risen Jesus—called out to them to cast their net on the right side of the boat. The net instantly filled with fish, and from this miracle the disciples recognized their master.

Bible commentators have long puzzled over this number. The British scholar John Michell recognized that the numbers 153 and 7 (the number of disciples who went fishing) allow the construction of a geometric design that holds great cosmological significance in the gnostic or hermetic tradition—the so-called *vesica piscis* ("vessel of the fish"). This design, which probably originated with the Pythagoreans in the pre-Christian era, can be seen in many windows in old churches. For St. Augustine, the 153 fish were symbolic of the number of souls on earth who would be saved at the end of time. Michell observes: "It is a traditional practice among teachers of esoteric philosophy to set forth their doctrines in the guise of parables which amuse children, enrich popular mythology and, for those who understand the science of interpreting them, illustrate various cosmological processes."

~227~

THE 227 DISCIPLINARY FORMULAS OF BUDDHISM

Buddhism has a strong monastic tradition, which goes back directly to Gautama the Buddha. In the course of his ministry over forty-five years, he not only encouraged the mendicant life but also instituted numerous rules for its guidance. Although just prior to his death the Buddha reputedly relieved his followers from the obligation to strictly adhere to even the minor rules, his monastic community opted to maintain all rules, perhaps because the monks were in some cases disputing whether a rule was major or minor.

The monk's life is governed by the precepts of what is called *patimokkha* in the Pali language (*pratimoksha* in Sanskrit). This is the basic monastic code, which every monk (and nun) must aspire to observe, without exception.

A person is eligible to be initiated as a monk (*bhikshu*) at the age of twenty. He must be free from certain physical ailments and occupational impediments, and he must have undergone a period of instruction by a senior monk. At a formal ceremony, the novice is proposed by his tutor to the assembly of monks (a quorum of at least ten monks is required). Acceptance must be unanimous.

During the ordination, the novice solemnly repeats the three refuges of Buddhism and then receives the ten principal monastic precepts out of a total of 227 (or, in some schools, 263): abstinence from the destruction of life, theft, fornication, lying, alcoholic drink, eating meals at forbidden times, social entertainment (such as dancing and singing), adorning the body, using a high or large seat, and receiving gold or silver.

The monastic rules are gathered in a special collection known as the "basket of disciplines" (*vinaya-pitaka*), which forms one of the three "baskets" of the Buddhist canonical literature. Here every rule of the pratimoksha code is explained and illustrated by a story, and the commentary also includes sophisticated legalistic discussions for some of the rules.

The nuns, who were allowed into the Buddhist monastic community as an afterthought, are obliged to follow a more extensive code, containing no fewer than 279 (or, in some schools, 380) disciplinary rules.

Any violation of these rules must be confessed at the fortnightly *uposatha* ("fasting") ceremony, at which the entire pratimoksha code is recited. The purpose of all these regulations is not to curtail a person's freedom but to liberate the Buddha's followers from the trammels of the ego. This spirtual purpose is captured in the Sanskrit word *pratimoksha,* which is derived from the verbal root *muc,* or "to release."

~ 231 ~

THE 231 GATES OF THE KABBALAH

The *Sefer Yetzirah* ("Book of Creation"), the oldest Kabbalistic work, states that God arranged the twenty-two "foundation letters" of the Hebrew alphabet in a circle, which was like a wall with 231 gates.

The 231 gates represent the total number of combinations of two letters of the Hebrew alphabet. Some Kabbalists have discovered this number in the name "Israel" (spelled *Yesh rla,* meaning literally "there are 231"). Kabbalists use this archetypal pattern in their rituals. They "carve" the twenty-two letters in the ground, either actually or merely in their mental visualization. The next step in this exercise is to draw the 231 connecting links, so that they form a protective dome above one. This practice has the dual purpose of achieving deep levels of meditation or conjuring up spirits.

Tradition has it that several disciples of the twelfth-century Kabbalist Rabbi Yitzchak ben Asher performed this ritual to create a golem. However, they chanted the alphabet in the wrong sequence and merely succeeded in sinking waist-deep into the earth. When their teacher heard of their failure, he instructed other disciples to recite the alphabet in the reverse order to free the unfortunate students.

An old tradition knows of 221 rather than 231 gates, connecting the former number to the number the Talmudic prophecy that King David's cup will hold 221 measures.

~ 260 ~

THE 260 DAYS OF THE
SACRED MAYAN CALENDAR

"As above, so below." This maxim, which is attributed to
Hermes Trismegistus, is fundamental to the metaphysical
thinking of all spiritual traditions: The regularities of the
celestial domain served as the archetypal pattern for human life on earth. Thus, early on, the spiritual pathmakers
of humanity looked to the heavens for guidance. This led
to the creation of sacred calendars, which furnished the
early cultures with a temporal framework for their most
significant rituals and ceremonies.

The Maya of Mexico, whose earliest history is still
unknown but who are now dated back to the second millennium B.C., were particularly skilled in astronomy and
calendrical science. They had an all-consuming interest in
time and time keeping. Thus they developed no fewer than
five calendars, which all had great practical importance.

The first is a solar calendar of 365.2425 days, which
is astonishingly correct, diverging from modern calculations by only .003 days! The second calendar is based on
an ideal year of 360 days (18 months × 20 days), while the
third calendar is calculated on the 584 days, which is the
synodical period of the planet Venus. The fourth calendar

is based on the lunar month of 29.5302 days (diverging from modern calculations by a mere 0.0003 days).

Finally, the fifth calendar recognizes a cycle of 260 days. This sacred calendar, which is known as *tzolkin,* and is still used by some contemporary Mayas, is really a divinatory almanac. It assigns to each day a particular quality, or energy, which results in good or ill fortune.

In the past, the temple priests were consulted to determine the most auspicious day for a wedding, business transaction, crop planting, or ceremony. Today it is the elders of a local community.

Each day is represented by (and personified as) a particular deity and is given a particular number. There are twenty days/deities and thirteen numbers (from 1 to 13). The twenty days/deities are: Imix (pronounced "Imish"), Ik, Akbal, Kan, Chicchan, Cimi, Manik, Lamat, Muluc, Oc, Chuen, Eb, Ben, Ix (pronounced "Ish"), Men, Cib, Caban, Eznab, Cauac, and Ahau.

The tzolkin calendar begins with 1 Imix and proceeds to 2 Ik, 3 Akbal, and so on, until 13 Ben. Then, because only the first thirteen numerals are employed, the fourteenth day is reckoned as 1 Ix, which is followed by 2 Men, 3 Cib, and so on, until 7 Ahau. The next twenty-day cycle begins 8 Imix. After 260 cycles, the opening day name is again 1 Imix.

The Maya were also keenly interested in how the sacred calendar and the solar calendar intermesh, and they calculated that together the two calendars form a 52-year cycle, which was given tremendous significance in religion. It is known as the "calendar round," and at the end of such a cycle the Maya extinguished their fires, smashed their earthen pots, fasted, and no doubt engaged in bloodletting. It was a time of dangerous transition and renewal.

THE 500 ARHATS OF BUDDHISM

Before the rise of Mahayana Buddhism, the Buddhist community celebrated the *arhats* ("worthy ones") as embodying the highest expression of spiritual life apart from the Buddha himself. The arhats, or *arhants,* were saints who had successfully followed the noble eightfold path of Buddhism to its end—attaining the state of *nirvana.*

An arhat is someone who (1) is indifferent to worldly things and inwardly free; (2) understands the nature of the five aggregates (i.e., physical form, sensation, perception, predisposition, and consciousness); (3) has no sense of "I," "me," or "mine"; (4) has no attachment to the sensory world; and (5) fully understands the conditioned origination of everything. An arhat also knows his previous births and the rebirths of others.

In India, during the early post-Christian era, the ideal of the arhat became largely replaced by that of the bodhisattva, the compassionate "enlightenment being" dedicated to the alleviation of suffering in others. By contrast, in Far Eastern Buddhism, especially the Ch'an (Zen) school, the figure of the arhat (called *lohan* in Chinese and *rakan* in Japanese) continued to inspire the monastic and the lay tradition. Here the arhats were venerated as saints who had attained liberation through their own efforts.

Many Chinese and Japanese monasteries contain statues of 500 arhats. The images are often arranged in groups of sixteen or eighteen in the central complex of the monasteries. They commemorate the 500 arhats who are said to have been present at the first Buddhist Council, which was convened shortly after the Buddha's death in order to fix the canonical teachings. Numerous legends have been woven around these venerated figures, and according to one tradition, they are said to live in 500 caves in the K'un-lun Mountains.

There also exists a tradition of 108 arhats, which likewise suggests comprehensiveness and completeness.

~ 613 ~

THE 613 COMMANDMENTS IN JUDAISM

The Torah ("Teaching") gives out no fewer than 613 commandments (*mitzvot*; singular *mitzvah*), including 248 positive rules and 365 prohibitions. The rabbinical commentaries on the Torah mention that the 248 positive rules correspond to the number of bones in the body (according to Aristotle's reckoning), whereas the 365 negative rules correspond to the number of days in the year. The hidden significance of these correspondences supposedly is that our bones demand of us to observe a positive mitzvah with them, whereas the days demand that we do not sin on them.

In contrast to the ten commandments, which were given by Yahweh directly to the people of Israel, the other commandments were communicated to Moses alone when he heard God's voice in the burning bush. But they all are equally binding, demanding great care, since a seemingly minor commandment may be major from the divine point of view.

However, there is considerable room for interpretation about how the commandments are to be understood in a practical context. For instance, the mitzvah to say a blessing before eating a meal does not specify exactly what is meant by a meal. Should a snack be considered a meal? Or tasting a piece of chocolate? Over the centuries the rabbis have invested much ingenuity and time in answering such detailed questions. Their deliberations are encoded in the rabbinic law, which is known as *halakha* ("way").

The commandments and their rabbinic explanations and additions cover the entire range of personal and social life. The observation of these numerous rules places a considerable burden on pious individuals, and there is always the danger of sterile formalism without heart. Hence Jewish sages and thinkers have periodically emphasized the need to remain sensitive to the inner moral value of the commandments over against their external expression. As one Talmudic sage observed: "A sin committed with a good intention has a greater merit than a commandment performed without it."

SEE ALSO The Ten Commandments in the Judeo-Christian Tradition

~666~

THE 666 UNITS OF THE MAGICAL SQUARE OF THE SUN IN THE WESTERN HERMETIC TRADITION

The Western hermetic tradition originated with Pythagoras, who was inspired by the Egyptians. In this tradition, sacred geometry was of paramount importance. One of the great mathematical mysteries concerned the magical square of the sun, consisting of the numbers 1 to 36, arranged in rows and columns of six numbers each, as follows:

6	32	3	34	35	1
7	11	27	28	8	30
19	14	16	15	23	24
18	20	22	21	17	13
25	29	10	9	26	12
36	5	33	4	2	31

Each row and each column adds up to 111, making a total of 666 for the magical square. This number was considered symbolic of the sun as the solar spirit, animating our universe. In St. John's Book of Revelation, or Apocalypse, the number 666 is associated with "the Beast." What John, who was deeply steeped in the gnostic tradition, failed to explain was that the fiery masculine principle of the sun is destructive only on its own. In conjunction with the feminine principle of the moon, as epitomized in the number 1080 (a multiple of 108), it is creative of life. The sum of both numbers, namely 1746, was thought to symbolize the universal spirit, the source of all feminine and masculine processes in Nature. Thus the evil connotation attributed to the number 666 is based on misunderstanding of the profound symbolism of the hermetic tradition.

SEE ALSO The Two Beasts of the Apocalypse in Christianity

THE 1,000 NAMES OF THE DIVINE IN HINDUISM

In Hinduism, as in many other spiritual traditions, the Divine is thought to transcend name (*nama*) and form (*rupa*). Yet, acknowledging the human need to worship a more tangible reality, Hindu theologians and mystics have given the Divine numerous names and forms. There even is a whole genre within the sacred Sanskrit literature that specializes in naming the Unnamable. The works in this literary category are known as "Thousand Names (of God)" (*Sahasra-Nama*).

Thus there are works by this title dedicated to the Divine in the form of Shiva, Vishnu, and the elephant-headed Ganapati (Ganesha), as well as in the form of the Goddess Lalita, and so on. These sacred texts are simply compilations of a thousand names celebrating particular characteristics of a given deity, many of which could apply equally to other deities. However, some of the names derive from the mythology that has evolved around such figures as Shiva, Vishnu, Ganesha, or Lalita.

Each name is considered a *mantra,* or sacred sound. The names should be uttered with great reverence only by those who are filled with devotion (*bhakti*) for the particular God or Goddess. According to the *Lalita-Sahasra-Nama,* which celebrates the Divine Mother, the Goddess has millions of names, but the selected 1,000 names are deemed the most excellent. They should be recited daily, either aloud or silently. This practice is said to gladden the heart of the Goddess and make her inclined to shower multiple blessings on her devotee, so that he or she may prosper spiritually.

According to some schools, the 1,000 names are associated with the 1,000 petals of the lotus flower that represents the psychospiritual center (*cakra*) at the crown of the head. This center is known as the *sahasrara-cakra*—from *sahasra* meaning "thousand" and *ara* meaning "spoke," while the term *cakra* literally means "wheel." This notion is probably derived from clairvoyant experience of the topmost psychospiritual center of the human body, which resembles so many filaments of light extending upward into infinity. It is here that, in Tantrism and Yoga, consciousness must ascend in order to achieve union with the ultimate Reality.

~ 5,000 ~

THE 5,000 LOAVES OF BREAD IN CHRISTIANITY

Like the allegory of the 153 fish in Christianity, the well-known gospel story of the feeding of the multitude of 5,000 contains a hidden symbolic and geometric message. According to the Gospel of Mark, Jesus and his disciples gathered in a remote place to rest from their busy life of preaching and ministering. However, some people recognized them and soon they were surrounded by a crowd of 5,000. Since it was getting late, Jesus wanted to feed all of them. But the disciples had brought only five loaves of bread and two fish.

Jesus asked everyone to sit down in groups by hundreds and by fifties. Then he blessed the food, placed it in twelve baskets, and divided the provisions among all the people. "And all ate and were filled."

As in the case of the 153 fish, the story of the feeding of 5,000 contains arithmetic clues that permit the construction of a sacred geometric design—that of a twelve-petaled flower. The total measure of the petals' arcs is 888, which, in the hermetic tradition, is the symbolic number of Jesus as the personified solar *logos* (the primordial

"Word"). This revealing interpretation of an otherwise puzzling story can be found in David Fideler's book *Jesus Christ Sun of God*. He writes: "On the outer level, the feeding of the five thousand was a delightful tale used by the early Christian missionaries to entertain their hearers and impress upon them the miraculous powers of the saving Word. On the inner level, however, the feeding of the five thousand provides nearly inexhaustible food for thought, for it is based on the Greek canon of number which was already old when Christianity was new."

~ 21,600 ~

THE 21,600 SILENT RECITATIONS OF THE
SOUL IN HINDUISM

According to a medieval Hindu teaching, the human soul spontaneously makes the sound *hamsa* 21,600 times every day and night. This spontaneous recitation is known as the *ajapa-mantra* or "nonrecitation sound," because it is not consciously produced, as in the case of mantric recitation (*japa*). Another designation is *hamsa-mantra*. The Sanskrit word *hamsa* means "swan" and here stands for the psyche, or soul (*jiva*), which animates the body through the breath.

The 21,600 recitations are none other than the body's automatic inhalations and exhalations by which the external air or *prana* is drawn into the body and then expelled again, after rejuvenating its organs and structures. The yogis think of the inhaled air as the coarse aspect of a more subtle energy, the prana, which they experience as rushing up and down in the body—rather like a swan in flight might climb too high only to drop to lower altitudes again. Breathing creates the sound *ham-sa, ham* being related to inhalation and *sa* to exhalation.

From a yogic point of view, however, the continuous

sound *hamsahamsahamsa* should be thought as consisting of *sa* ("he") and *ham,* standing for *aham* ("I"): *so'ham* or "I am He." Thereby the soul is said to affirm its essential identity with the Divine. This nondualist teaching is fundamental to the tradition of Hatha-Yoga—an approach to Self-realization that seeks to transmute the human body primarily through the control of the life force (prana) and its outermost manifestation, the breath. The breath is regarded as the vehicle for mental concentration. By harmonizing, deepening, and lengthening the breathing cycle, the mind becomes calm and focused and thus is rendered fit to perceive its anchorage in the transcendental Self (*atman*).

~144,000~

THE 144,000 SAVED SOULS IN CHRISTIANITY

In his end-time vision, as so vividly described in the Apocalypse (14:1), St. John mentions that he saw a lamb standing on Mount Zion, accompanied by 144,000 humans. They had the "Father's" name written on their foreheads, and were listening to the thunderous voice from heaven and were learning a new song of the heavenly liturgy from the angels.

The Mount Zion mentioned by St. John is not the earthly mountain but a sacred elevated place outside heaven in which the Messiah appears at the end of time. Here the elect few, who bear the seal of God on their foreheads, are gathered. They are the men and women who are without sin, who did not follow the evil ways of the Beast. St. John speaks of them as not having been "defiled by women" and as "virgins," though this is generally understood in a metaphoric sense, and thus not exclusive of the female gender.

The lamb (Greek *arnion*) in St. John's vision is none other than the Christ himself, this being a favorite expression of the apostle who authored the Gospel of John. This idea perhaps goes back to the time of the prophet Isaiah who likened the servant of God to a lamb. In the Aramaic language, the word *talya* means both "servant" and "lamb." In ancient biblical times, the lamb was a principal victim in sacrifices. Jesus' suffering on the cross and total obedience to the will of God suggested to the early Christian mind the image of the lamb that innocently allows itself to be led to the altar where it is sacrificed.

There has been much discussion among scholars and the clergy over the identity of those 144,000 elect souls, but no definite conclusion has emerged. What is certain from St. John's eschatological vision is that all others are condemned to much purification and perhaps even have to face the dread prospect of eternal damnation.

We need not take the number given by St. John literally, however. At a time when there were as yet few Christians in the world, and the population of our planet was around 170 million people, three percent of what it is now, 144,000 may have seemed a reasonably large number. Today, 144,000 seems a small number even within the Christian community, which now, on the North American continent alone, is as large as the world population was at the time of Jesus. Be that as it may, many Christians find consolation in the following belief, expressed in the Gospel of John (6:35):

> I am the bread of life; whoever comes to me will never hunger; and whoever believes in me will never thirst.

~ ABOUT THE AUTHOR ~

Georg Feuerstein, Ph.D., is a historian of religion, specializing in Hinduism and the Yoga tradition in particular. His over twenty books include the award-winning *Encyclopedic Dictionary of Yoga; Holy Madness; Sacred Sexuality;* and *The Mystery of Light.* After a quarter of a century of research into a variety of Hindu teachings, he is currently studying and practicing the Healing Buddha tradition of Tibetan Buddhism under the guidance of Lama Shakya Zangpo.